The Unbearable Wrongness of Being

The Unbearable Wrongness of Being

Exploring and Getting Beyond the Myth of Unhappiness

Frank Mosca Ph.D.

Writers Club Press
San Jose New York Lincoln Shanghai

The Unbearable Wrongness of Being
Exploring and Getting Beyond the Myth of Unhappiness

Writers Club Press
an imprint of iUniverse.com, Inc.

For information address:
iUniverse.com, Inc.
5220 S 16th, Ste. 200
Lincoln, NE 68512
www.iuniverse.com

ISBN: 0-595-17173-7

Printed in the United States of America

To Roedi Reeberg, my fellow traveler on the road to happiness.

Contents

Prologue and Acknowledgements

Gentle Reader, this book makes no promises! If you read it and apply all that you could know from so doing, there are no guarantees that somehow, mystically, mysteriously, you will attract wealth, influence, power; that you will grow bulging muscles or discover the nutritional key to a healthy life. No, ALL that you could discover in this book is HAPPINESS, that it is your birthright, that it is the very essence of who you are NOW without going one word further.

Additionally, there are no miracles displayed within these pages, unless you will accept the miracle of yourself, of your own happiness, and of the potential miracle of happiness that can await you. Know then, that if you seek miracles, that that alone awaits you, the MIRACLE OF YOURSELF, of the happy you, free from all conditions and encumbrances, to be that way forever!

For that miracle, I am grateful to the person who discovered the truth about happiness some decades ago, Bruce Di Marsico. His vision has been a transformational catalyst for me and for others, so that we too could know our happiness without reserve, if we so chose. My gratitude goes also to my friend Roedi Reeberg who made me aware of Bruce's existence. Our friendship has spanned many years and it is to him that I dedicate this book. Many thanks old friend.

Chapter One

Introduction

The Pursuit of Happiness

Happiness, a straightforward word for what seems for many like an elusive felt experience. Sure, most know what it means. Laughing at a friend's joke, your girlfriend acknowledging she likes you, the smile of your first-born child, a bonus at work, a good meal, slipping into bed with that heavy fatigue about to be so sweetly dissolved in comforting sleep. So, what's the problem? Well, all the endless ways in which we can experience happiness are truly exciting. However, for most, these moments are but islands of reprieve in the larger sea of anxieties and concerns.

What's more, that larger sea seems, at times at least, to dwarf the smaller land masses of good feelings; sometimes the storms that whip up threaten to engulf our equanimity completely and leave us totally devastated. We are told that this is the natural ebb and flow of being human. The best we can hope for is a flexible adaptation to the shifting sands of fate that we are told determine our experience of the world.

It is 'natural,' we are told, and more importantly *we actually feel* ourselves to be in varying states of distress as the world presents us with its endless dilemmas. When we try to plumb the world's religions and philosophies for remedies, we are led on a curious path. In the West, the responses begin with describing our state as the result of the 'initial conditions' of the choices our primal parents made in the Garden of Eden. They 'blew it' for all of us, and forever we must bear the burden of their guilt. The promise and the solution given exist only outside of time in an afterlife where the conditions of absolute equanimity will reign undisturbed forever. But as for now, well, your suffering is actually 'good for you' because it can teach you to avoid the even greater evils that might deprive you of the promised eternal place of solace.

In the East, the problem of unhappiness is addressed as an outcome of individuality. It is the "I" through its wants, desires, needs that fixes us in the pain of individual life. What we could come to know, according to this version, is that by understanding that individual life is actually an illusion, we can surrender our "I" and all its attendant miseries and attain to the utter indifference of the "all."

For those who find religions unappetizing for whatever reasons, there is a smorgasbord of rationales to help one explain why unhappiness seems so doggedly ubiquitous and persistent. Some have said, in a secular variant of the promise of Western religion, that human miseries are the outcome of cultural and social configurations; economic conditions determine consciousness. History is working its way out of these cruder, more painful phases and is heading towards resolution and clarification. For some adherents of such views, the resolution is through revolution. Humans are stimulus/response machines that require the proper environmental "tuning" through appropriate structure in a political/social sense. Even for those who do not see the need for revolution, the answers to the human dilemma are perhaps most often, if not always, couched in some form of manipulation of the world around. For, it has been forever hypothesized, if one can just find the right formula, theory, incantation, ritual, structure, or, as the flip side variant of the same view, if one can only rid the environment of the demon, devil, enemy, group, race, individual, etc., that is standing in the way of equanimity, then all would be well!

And yet, despite prayers, tears, fears, deaths beyond counting, enemies slaughtered without mercy, theories tried to the utmost, the same basic state of dis-ease remains rampant for humanity. Happiness eludes us except in fits and starts; even when it is present, other people, events, the mysterious gyres and whorls of the great unknowns of the universe threaten at any moment to descend upon us and snatch it away. Slender indeed is any hope for ongoing happiness and joy.

It is not for lack of trying that humans find themselves deprived somehow of the happiness they seek. More people than ever before, at least in the "advanced countries" of the West, have turned to the new "religions" of psychotherapy for solace. On innumerable couches, on mats, in gripping encounter sessions, people analyze, confront, scream, lend their bodies to the fiercest manipulations, surrender their wills to a higher power, pursue their "inner children" with unfettered tenderness, gladly confess the "sins" of codependence, willingly undergo the often violent exorcisms of suppressed child abuse—all at the hands of the new priests of a new age and all in the pursuit of the elusive butterfly of happiness. The gurus of self-liberation and empowerment entrance audiences from sea to shining sea, gathering ever more lucrative tithes from the faithful seeking absolution from the "original sin" of being human and hoping to be lifted up and reborn into that state of bliss that is charismatically projected for a few hours by the intense minister of mental health up there on the stage.

Yes, there are gains, cures, changes, growth, improvements; people pass from passivity (some few, just enough to serve as agonizing exemplars of what can never be for the great mass of others) into a blinding array of activity. The revival tent is struck, the show moves on. People awake days or weeks or even years later to find that the same dull ache of anxiety and indecision hangs on. But, not to despair, yet another angel of insight is bound to be coming through making the rounds with a tempting bag of nostrums. Just look at the bulletin boards, the new age journals, the old age journals, the placards, the TV spots, the talk show guest circuits, salvation is never far from hand. You just got to believe, yes just believe!

Indeed, in this book belief will be the central theme. Am I just another "angel of insight," to quote myself? Well, that will be for you to decide when you complete this journey with me. For what I offer you unabashedly is an INVITATION TO HAPPINESS. Yes, that's right friends. Let me hear an "amen." Just kidding. Yes just kidding, because whimsy, play, the ability to live in the flow of the moment is a central feature of my story, or stories as they will turn out to be. And yet, that "invitation" that I speak of is both real, in the sense that I am going to be inviting you to know something that you more than likely do not know, but, at the same time, it is bogus, in the sense that what I am inviting you to know is something you already possess and once known do not need my help to experience at all!

The Unbearable Wrongness of Being

Sometime before 1970, a man with a background in religion, philosophy and psychology came to the remarkable conclusion that people did not have to be unhappy, they merely believed they had to be: *The cause of unhappiness is a belief. What happens, no matter how undesirable or destructive to our life, health, desires or loves, does not cause unhappiness. The belief that we have to be unhappy is the only cause. To state it simply: If a person did not believe he or she had to be unhappy, they would not and could not be. We merely believe we need to have things or avoid things in order to avoid unhappiness, which we would not have to fear if we did not believe we needed to be unhappy.* (Bruce Di Marsico, 1970)1

This insight, soon developed into a method of self-awareness, was termed by him the Option Method. The use of the word Option simply denotes the central place that choice plays in the unfolding of human life and its power to alter utterly how that life is experienced. The title of this book is derived from his alteration of the title of the book by the Czech writer Milan Kundera entitled the *Unbearable Lightness of Being*. What I am referring to are the basic assumptions about life, an experience I will later term Primal Dread, and how they can and do lead humans to conclude that life itself, being in all its variety is *unbearable*. This book is an elaboration of Bruce Di Marsico's extraordinary self-revelation. It does not purport to represent his views exactly, only he can do that; but there is no question that his views, as will be represented in quotations throughout this text, are the essential inspiration for my present work. His words, to the degree they will be present, will speak for him, as mine will for me. It is my hope that they will be experienced by the reader as producing a synergy of information that will open hearts to the ground state of happiness that is all that there is.

Now, it is not that people do not want to be happy. Quite the opposite, as my earlier introduction indicates, people are expending and have expended enormous energies in the pursuit of happiness, a pursuit that has often led to the very opposite of happiness as religious and ideological systems structured themselves into repressive, rigid, often pale reflections of sometimes refreshing and promising original insights. Humankind seems often to leap from one expression of that pursuit to another, in sometimes violent paradoxical swings that are designed somehow to engineer bliss into the human equation. No one, though, until Bruce Di Marsico arrived at his insight, had, in my opinion, defined as clear a vision of either happiness, or how it could be achieved and maintained. This book is dedicated to an exploration of that fundamental insight through fictional dialogues, the nature of which I will describe in a while. First, let me review a few key notions that will lay the groundwork, both for understanding the concept and of applying it in your own life.

Belief: That Which Is Beloved

The core meaning of belief is akin to beloved, that which we love. What we love we are congruent with in the sense of striving to reflect that love in all we do. Beliefs are our operative realities. In a crude sense, they are like the programs in a computer. Each program operates according to certain rules, a certain internal logic in order to produce whatever effect the program is designed to produce. Once you are in the "logic envelope" of the program, you can only operate according to the rules of the program. Unless you are a computer programmer, you never look at the logic or the rules. They operate out of your immediate awareness; what you see are the results of the program as it responds to your input according to the rules:

Unhappiness is a belief alone. It is the belief alone which makes the person experience what seems like unhappiness to herself/himself. If there is anything we know to be wrong it is the belief that is held by the person, not the suffering human. The belief in evil and unhappiness is not wrongfully held, the belief is what is wrong. It is held like humans are rightfully able to hold any belief they believe in.2

These are the accumulations of our perceptions of the world since the beginning of our lives. They are woven from the fabric of the world around us, because we are part of the larger webs of interactivity that present us with different kinds of information in a vast variety of ways every second of our lives. That information comes to us with different shades of bias. By that I mean that our culture defines the world and its issues in a certain way. Then our society on all its levels filters and modifies the general cultural message in ever more specific layers of interaction. Finally, our family, in the person of what is now termed "significant others" is the most immediate mediator of the information extant in the world around.

We respond first in the tiny orbit of our immediate family. In this close and intense environment we are given a total immersion in the beliefs of our parenting figures. What they believe becomes at least in tentative form what we believe. We have no reason to believe anything else, since our knowledge of what is is limited by our home and our neighborhood; only later does it widen out to include schools, organized religion, people and institutions of varying kinds, depending on our own special circumstances of upbringing.

The pursuit of happiness is there from the beginning. Better to say, HAPPINESS IS THE ORIGINAL CONDITION OF OUR BEING AND REMAINS SO UNTIL WE ARE GIVEN REASONS BY OTHERS, AND THEN ULTIMATELY BY OURSELVES, TO BELIEVE OTHERWISE. We know that we were indeed given reasons to be unhappy from the earliest moments of our lives. Our parents modeled for us their version of the cultural myth as they came to know it. Whatever was idiosyncratic about how they enacted that myth in their lives, one dimension was certain: they believed that other people were responsible, had the power, to create feelings in them and they believed in evil, good/bad etc.

Wanting: Bane or Bliss

"I do not understand my own actions. For I do not do what I want, but I do the very thing I hate." Romans.7.15

Therefore, with mother's milk so to speak, came the entire program of pseudo-causality (others creating states of feeling in us) and good/bad. When our parents would become enraged, cry, be depressed, we observed and saw how these states were used in the interplay of human behavior. We saw that anger seemed to get people what they wanted or move others to get what we want; that becoming unhappy would sometimes get others to feel bad for us, and that could get us what we wanted. Of course, such manoeuvres backfired in many instances as often as they worked. We learned that if we feigned crying to get what we wanted, we might also get a negative response, a reprimand, a yell or physical punishment. So, fear became attached to wanting; mere wanting was not enough. People around us were not acting as if they wanted things. Rather they were acting as if they "needed" things; further, if they didn't get the things they needed, then "naturally" they would be unhappy. We saw for them as for us, when we adopted the "need" concept that many times we simply were not going to get what we "needed" and hence, unhappiness was unavoidable.

What we could not know, but what was soon to be part of what we believed, was that our parents and the world around were dealing with the issue of CONTROL. The technology of control, whether it be religious, ideological, scientific, psychological etc., is the core concern of humankind. For, since humans believe that the world around creates all inner states of experience (even those systems that purport to believe otherwise always fall short of true, full human autonomy), then the issue comes to be the *oughtness* or *shouldness* quotient of the world, that is, the degree to which the world corresponds to the way we come to believe *it has to be* in order for us to be happy!

And so, at the deepest level, people are not unhappy about not getting what they want, but more nearly about WHAT THAT MEANS ABOUT THEM! Our happiness is always in doubt and we can often be on the edge of experiencing the "unbearable wrongness of being." We need the world to be the way we say it ought to be so that we can feel the way we should feel, so that we can be the way we want to be, that is happy:

People want everyone to be kind and loving so that they (the people) don't have to hate anyone. If you say you need to love all humankind, therefore everyone must be lovable. All depends on their behavior because only their behavior can deprive you of what you want: I hate you because by being who you are I can't love you.3

Thus we fear wanting, not only because we fear not getting what we want, but also when we don't, it must mean that the world is not the way it ought to be and that there is something wrong with our wanting itself. Since we cannot know all there is to know about the world, then how do we know that what we want is all right for us to want? Perhaps what we want is bad for us and therefore our wanting is "wrong". Thus, we acquire the obsession, the need to control all that there is before the elusive notion of happiness could ever possibly become a reality. The inner belief that wanting is wrong is the main precipitating factor in creating the experience of the "unbearable wrongness of being."

First, though, returning to our evolution from childhood, we had to pass out of the phase of merely utilizing the information around us as a tool for negotiating our way through life. After innumerable repetitions of our repertoires of crying, screaming, nagging, sulking etc., in the service of our "needs" we gradually let the whole understanding that this was simply a strategy slip out of our awareness. After all, the adults around us were not acting. They were absolutely congruent with what they were feeling and consequently with the behaviors that followed. There was no one to tell us otherwise, so the primal knowledge that human emotions are a function of how we shape them slowly ebbed and faded into our own acceptance of the belief that we no longer had that knowledge. Now we were pretending that we never had pretended in the first place. Once inside the logic envelope of that second level of pretense, we lost touch with our original intuitions about the nature of being human. We were doubly dissociated, to use a term employed in the language of alternative states of mind.

Again, we now take those original strategies that we learned from observing our parents in their living out, acting out, their unhappiness, and make them "real". While, before, they were just part of our world of pretense, ways of getting us what we wanted. True, they were deviations from our natural state of equanimity, or happiness, but, they were what others around us were doing, so we dealt with what we had. Then, at some indeterminate point, we step over the line into acting as if the act was not an act but the true state of how things are. Just imagine, we go into a movie and for several hours, we act as if something real were taking place. The images on the screen are projected and we allow that information to be processed in roughly the same way we would outside the theater. That is, if it is a "horror" movie, should we so choose, we might feel dread, revulsion and so on, but always with the realization that this is "only a movie" and what is being presented is after all not really taking place. This is the "willing suspension of disbelief" that allows us to "enjoy" such "as if" circumstances as a movie, a play etc. Now, the level of our feelings may be intense, BUT, again, we KNOW that we are only pretending! We can produce feelings in such situations, but they are very like the feelings we produced when we played as children.

We all remember how intense our games could be, but we all came out of our roles when we heard our mothers calling us for supper. Remember, a "sore loser" was someone who could not handle the pretence and for a variety of reasons took the game to be "real" and invested that belief in the process of the game. Such people were not well liked because they had not the flexibility to move comfortably from within the shell of the game with its attendant "real" emotions to the outside experience, where such emotions simply would not exist. This is even more so the case where people would take a movie to be real and remain "locked in" to the logic of the fiction "as if" it were reality to them. Such people we identify as "psychotic"; that is, they believe and respond to things which we define as clearly fictional in some way, i.e., as not having any ontological status. If someone says that they are being controlled by "voices from Mars," we may indulgently chuckle at the absurdity of such an idea. Note, that our explanation of the "madness" is strictly centered on the improbability of the "voices from Mars" angle. If a wife says to a husband: "you have made my life miserable," we do not treat that in the same way, even though there is no essential difference between the two! Both are saying that other people/forces have been able to create feelings within them. The only question at hand is perhaps the intensity of the control and the believability of the source of control—a husband we believe in, voices from Mars we do not.

Belief, then is that which feels congruent. It would have to, otherwise it wouldn't be believed! Bruce notes "you cannot be unhappy about something that you are not afraid of." Which is to say, that the correspondence between belief and feeling is absolute.

When someone is depressed and you inquire why they would feel the way they feel, they may meet you with a blank stare. While, as we will see, they do have reasons and many times will be able to articulate them in some initial way, as per the Option Method, they still would insist that they just feel that way! If you ask them to think of times when they felt another way, they will perhaps acknowledge that they did, but at this moment, all they know is what they feel now. Most times, it is difficult, if not impossible for them to imagine feeling another way unless and until the truth about their relation to themselves, that seamless tie between belief and feeling, is exposed. Then, they could know that the state of feeling is not in any way an absolute and inevitable organizer of our experiential destinies.

When we come into the knowledge of our position as self creators, we could know that a change of mind state, a *metanoia*, is but an instant away if we choose it. Believing that a change of mind is inacessible locks us into the puzzling status of being so desperately helpless before our feelings. This is despite our lifelong sense that we no longer believe or in any way are attached to a whole host of beliefs we formerly held with intense passion earlier in our lives, i.e., our belief in Santa Klaus, or some religious, political or ideological perspective or prejudice. We cannot find a trace of this emotion in our being and, yet, we know, remember clearly, being so rooted in intensity around that particular belief.

In a jocular vein, I recall my daughters upon occasion, when they were teenagers, declaring with great drama and vehemence that should the designated great passion of the week not call or take them to the dance, etc. that they would simply "die." When I might dare to question the authenticity of such emphatic exclamations, I was greeted by deep sighs of disbelief at my insensitivity along with the slamming of doors.

Further, one person whom I had helped get over very severe panic attacks when she was in her early teen years, came a decade later to seek help with a budding relationship. The theme was akin to "if he leaves me I will die." I pointed to the street corner where years ago, she absolutely believed that if she were to cross the street, she would either die or go stark raving mad with panic, so intense and unarguable were the severity of her feelings. Then I asked her please to feel as if she were going to die if she crossed the street. She looked at me with some alarm and puzzlement and responded that that was simply impossible, that she had not, and could not find within her any such feelings of doom about crossing a street anymore. To which I replied, that's right, now what about your boyfriend's rejecting you makes you believe that you would die? This was the beginning of a fruitful dialogue on the road to coming into possession of the truth about her beliefs.

Now we can begin to appreciate the power of belief as the primary shaper of our experience. What we believe, we feel and what we feel we believe! To reiterate it, from the Option founder's perspective:

Therefore, the beginning point, the Great Truth we start with, is that we know that people believe that unhappiness is necessary, and that is why they are unhappy., they believe they must be unhappy and are suffering because they believe it is an inescapable truth. Unhappiness is simply believing; not being, or getting ,or making, or doing unhappiness.4

A World Without Judgements

This brings us to another facet of belief. Remember, as a result of our "cultural trance" we now see "good and evil" as real entities, as the root duality that has to be addressed. Now when you have a duality, then there is the necessity of defining and distinguishing the one from the other. So from the outset, the tribes of humans would divide themselves and all other things into those that were either "good" or "bad." There were many levels of bad and many words to define those levels. The process of this definition making is called judging or being judgmental. It attributes bad or evil motives to those people who are doing things we would want them not to do. The child who is not doing what she is told is described as "bad," meaning she's not doing what others want her to do. But "bad" is something, again, as we mentioned earlier, that is given the status of objective reality and, therefore, something that we want to avoid.

Thus, the child wants to lose the status of bad as soon as possible and return to the status of "good." Loving is tied to the notions of bad and good. With the bad, love disappears or diminishes, with the good, love is given. So judging is used as a motivator in many instances to get "bad" people to become "good" people. Of course one person's bad may be another person's good. One can also talk of a kind of in-between neutral state where people, events, things are neither good nor bad, but few experiences escape the coloration of judgement. When there is not agreement on what is good or bad, then people, a child, for example, can be caught in a crossfire of judgements and counter-judgements, i.e., as in divorce situations where each parent wants the child to pledge allegiance to them and to validate their judgements of the other parent as "bad." This constant cacophony of judging in a world where the relativism of the judging becomes all too apparent can lead to a deep cynicism on the one hand or a very narrow "fundamentalism" on the other. The search for certainty about right or wrong, good or evil can manifest itself in the certainty of the cynical, who know that it's ALL bullshit and thereby lump everyone in the trash barrel of hypocrisy. It can also manifest itself in the certainty of the "righteous" who purport to know in very exact and unwavering terms what right and wrong are. The righteous are thereby compelled by their knowledge to give over their energies to an ongoing discrimination among these factors in ever more minute and obscure interpretations to cover every possible case.

But, we could come to know that judging is totally unnecessary when we understand that the premise on which it rests has no validity. We are all doing the best we can, given what we know, i.e, believe. If we knew to do otherwise, that is, believed otherwise, then we would do so. So what is there to judge!

But, let me emphasize, that knowing there is nothing to judge in no way disempowers you from creating consequences for others who act against your best interests. In such cases you might well have recourse to the judicial mechanisms of society for control and protection. Now, I am fortunate enough to live in one of the freest societies presently in existence. I relish and enjoy the freedom and latitude that being in such a society allows, even though, there are many aspects of this society that I personally do not agree with, or might want to be different. Still, I know that I freely choose to observe the laws, those that I find congenial and protective of my interests and wish enforced, and those that I find ill conceived or opposed to what I would prefer. I observe them to retain my "member in good standing" status as a reliable citizen and because I do not wish to incur consequences that would degrade the freedoms that I do enjoy and cherish. Thus, my not judging does not mean that I oppose the consequences that the community has arranged to protect its (and in many instances my) interests against those who might decide for their own reasons not to observe the legal and social arrangements that constitute this society. I do not have to judge such individuals as being "good" or "bad," but in many instances I am quite pleased that they are constrained by such consequences as obtain when they engage in those behaviors, particularly those that I find inimical to my personal well being.

Remember, to the degree you let go of judging, you liberate yourself! Judging self and others is a burden that you picked up from your experience with your parents, your culture etc. When locked into that posture, you feel compelled to criticize and judge in order to show that you are serious, that you care. Not to judge would stamp you as an unworthy person, or even as a bad person, depending upon the context:

You, and Everyone Else, Are Absolutely Innocent And Completely Forgiven For Everything. Let's make it simple. Whatever you have been, considering what you believed, and how you perceived things, you were being the way you were supposed to be. You couldn't have been different. If that helps you to understand your life it is because it is true. If that feels relieving, or like forgiveness that is because it is true. True forgiveness is knowing that there is nothing to forgive. There is no evil, and there was never anything that wasn't supposed to be, or was not allowed.5

Fear: a Metachronic State: How the Future Not the Past Can Control the Present

Fear, the word itself "strikes fear" into some of us. But what is it? Fear is the state of anticipating that something that is going to happen is going to be bad for us. That state of believing generates a state of feeling as part of the continuum of the belief process itself. Then a natural feedback loop is established, the "feared" future event is feared and the more it is feared, the more uncomfortable, unhappy and fearful you become about it. And so it goes on and on, depending upon the strength of the belief, until it can reach panic proportions.

Note, that the original assessment about the future event is never questioned in this cycle. Only the ways in which it will create some unhappiness in you by virtue of whatever it is. This cycle is embodied in the by now "old" joke about the person whose car breaks down and who lacks a wrench to fix it. Upon spying a nearby house the person then begins to hypothesize that the person within will probably not have a wrench and if they do will not lend it to them. Nevertheless, they move in the direction of the house, all the while building this negative, unhappy cycle of anticipation about the inevitable unhappy outcome and inevitable frustration and disappointment. By the time they reach the door, ring the bell and someone answers, this has built to the point that they don't even ask for what they want, but simply exclaim to the puzzled resident of the house, "You can keep your fucking wrench!"

In a sense, fear is a natural outcome of the belief in evil because, without the belief that there are forces"out there" that can create feeling states within us, we would negotiate our environment on the purely empirical basis that whatever worked for us was "good" and what did not was "bad," not in the sense of causing emotional discomfort, but just as a shorthand way of describing things that do or do not yield us what we want. But with evil comes the sense of the inevitability of things, people, events, places etc., that can harm us "against our will." Now, obviously, I am not talking about physical injury. Anyone or anything can inflict that intentionally or by accident. The external world is contingent, that is, ruled by the uncertainty principle, where each evolving moment is open to the micro and macro dynamics of the workings of the universe—that world is the way that it is, the laws of physics apply and we do not control its operations.

No, what we are addressing here, to reiterate, is the world of the self, the inner experience of who you are—that world is uniquely and utterly your own to define and operate as you negotiate your way through the universe in space and time. To speak of the self, the "I," one must understand the nature of our executive capacity. In order for it to exist at all, there has to be the right conjugation of forces, mental, physical, informational, concentrated in one place, what we call the human body. Tamper with that body beyond a certain point, and the self disappears. Thus, to talk of controlling others in any way is a fiction, if by control, you mean making others do what you want, or causing them to feel or think certain ways. All that can be done is to apply physical coercion to the body as a reality or a threat. One can use words to enhance the informational package to try to get others to do your will. One can use drugs or some other variant of physical coercion, but, again, employed beyond a certain point, all you have is the absence of the "I." Thus, the integrity of the self is absolute; it would have to be in order to be a "self" because that is exactly the nature of the self, to be itself utterly and without equivocation. The "I," the self can be destroyed, or at least, the physical vehicle for manifesting it can, but it cannot be "made" to do or feel anything but what it wants to. By "feel" here, of course, again I am speaking of "believing" in the sense mentioned earlier. I do not mean physical sensations which others will feel if we contact them.

The Structure of Believing: Review and Application of the Option Method.

So let us recap the main assertions of our book and of the Option Method. First, there is no such "thing" as unhappiness, but only the assertion, affirmation, hence belief/feeling that such a state exists. What there is, is only what is, that is reality. What is has no innate characteristics such as "good" or "bad" or "evil." Such descriptions could only apply in a personal, pragmatic way. For example, to stand in the street in the face of an oncoming truck could be seen by me as "bad" for me, if I have my physical survival in mind. Likewise, to eat foods that I believe to be appropriately nourishing I could see as being "good" for me in the sense of preserving my physical health.

Happiness is NOT the acceptance of what is, nor even of yourself, except in the sense that you know that there is nothing about you that causes you to have to be, or could make you be, unhappy. That being the case, there is nothing wrong with anything! Nor was there ever anything wrong, nor could there ever be. That in no way means that your liking of anything about the universe, others or even ourselves is required. Rather, it is knowing without reservation or condition that even if the whole of creation, including ourselves, were not to our liking, it would in no way deprive us of our happiness. We can be quite happy to know and, indeed, to revel in knowing that we like what we like and we do not like what we do not like.

Nothing, therefore, needs to be "fixed" about what is. There is no original sin, or primal fault, or fall from grace, or racial drive to dominance, or economic or ideological schema of any kind required to "fix" the world or any of its institutions, systems, cultures or any of the individuals who inhabit that world. There are only the practical problems that arise from differences in preference, all of which could be settled were it not that the vast majority of people are entranced into their own states of personal, cultural, religious, ideological imperatives. The attainment of these is required, since they are believed to be the vehicles of their meaning, the gateways to their happiness; additionally in a world where "evil" lurks as the *mysterium iniquitatis*, the outside force, however conceived, that can somehow deprive them of equanimity against their will, they seek power as an antidote to that fearful existential state of vulnerability and use power to strike out at and destroy the assumed evil persons or institutions that they see as the cause of their miseries.

Since happiness is in no way contingent, that is dependant upon any circumstance to be realized, it follows that wanting is not a problem but the open joy of experiencing life. Since getting what you want never involves your happiness, you are, as some would see it, paradoxically, totally free to want all you wish, whatever you wish. Without the burden of "needing" anything to complete or give meaning to your life in any instant of your existence, you can bring to bear in the service of your wanting the fullness that your creative intelligence will provide you in the exploration and invention of means to attain those wishes. Therefore, the affirmation of your happiness not only does not deprive you of your ability to move about in the world with acumen and zest, but it leavens your capabilities exponentially, because your desires are never clouded over with anxiety or a sense of being driven, but rather you engage life with a full, eager embrace, mindful only of the practical consequences of your attempts to achieve what you want. Thus, while there is nothing to fix in the world, that in no way means that you are somehow doomed to a vapid indifference or disconsolate non-attachment. Quite the contrary, your entry into the stream of reality can be purposeful and creative, blending your own self interests with the interests of others to create larger units of cooperation and consensus. After all, you probably will want a context, an environment that affords you the most freedom, latitude and security that you can attain. Therefore the principle of cooperation based on your self-interest can be a natural outcome of being happy.

The Method: the Quiddities

"the whatness of our whoness hath fetched his whenceness." (Joyce, *Ulysses*)

Having described the basic concepts of the Option approach to self and the world, the question arises, how do you attain to this perspective of ongoing happiness, or, more modestly, less and less unhappiness? Well, to begin with, what you will hopefully come to see is that the assumptive architecture of unhappiness is always basically the same. It is like a fractal in complex systems theory, where the image seen on any scale level may be quite different in appearance, but the underlying mathematical formula that produces the graphic representation is always the same.

So it is with unhappiness, as we have described it. In order to reveal this underlying construction, there are three basic questions, with unending variants, that can be asked to bring the hidden structure of unhappiness into conscious awareness. The first is WHAT ARE YOU UNHAPPY ABOUT? This question simply initiates the dialogue and in a neutral way requests that the person identify what they believe to be the issue of their unhappiness. The initial person, place or thing that is identified as the source of their unhappiness will only be the outer layer of the "onion" of unhappiness. As will be seen in the fictional dialogues that will follow in the chapters ahead, it only marks out a surface feature of the landscape of assumptions; much more is to follow.

Once having established the initial WHAT, we can go to the next question or any variant of it, which is WHAT ABOUT THAT MAKES YOU UNHAPPY?

This question engages the fundamental truth that what you are unhappy about is not actually why you are unhappy. Which is to say that they, you, believe that under the circumstances that constitute whatever the situation or issue in question, you have to be unhappy. This first step is apparently so simple, but is of major importance. Why? Because for so many, unhappiness just seems to "happen," just seems to arise automatically, organically out of the nature of the issue or situation without any reflection or thought whatsoever on their part. The word "happy" derives from the Old English "hap" or simply that which occurs, luck! Thus people see themselves as "hapless" or without any luck; just more evidence of the "unbearable wrongness of being" and their helplessness in the face of it. This is the experience of pseudo-causality that is so common to people and leads to the despair of "evil" or the mysterious arising of feelings within us that seem to appear against our will.

Thus, the answer to that question will begin a journey of self-revelation for the one who wants to be less unhappy. The reasons for unhappiness are endless, personal idiosyncratic takes on the larger streams of assumptions about life. "I am unhappy because my wife has left me," or "because she has decided to stay." "I am unhappy because I don't have enough money to buy happiness," or "I am unhappy because now that I have all the money I could want, I find that I cannot buy happiness." But, the answer will usually include the conjunction or preposition "because," "because of," which in itself is an admission that there is a reason for the unhappiness, albeit a reason believed, in most cases, to originate outside the person in some other person place or thing.

So, again, to ask WHY is to offer to the person an invaluable bit of knowing: however understood, their unhappiness results in some way from their understanding of the situation as being unhappy, and is not simply an eruption of misery into their lives from unknown sources. The third question is the one that peels back the final layer and reveals the truth about unhappiness, i.e., not only do we have a reason for our unhappiness, but that the reason itself is one that we have invented because of a fear of doing otherwise. So we ask WHAT ARE YOU AFRAID WOULD HAPPEN, OR WHAT ARE YOU AFRAID IT

WOULD MEAN, IF YOU WERE NOT UNHAPPY? That is, if you were not unhappy about whatever it is you are presently unhappy about.

Having been acculturated, and, hence, having chosen through our several levels of trance dissociation, to believe that unhappiness is inevitable, even necessary in our lives, we find ourselves in the strange position of yearning for happiness, but constantly coming up against situations that demand our unhappiness. Why is unhappiness required? That's because in all cultures, in the many different ways that this is expressed, our unhappiness is a sign of many things. Our outrage, anger is often taken as a sign of our sincerity, of our loyalty to a particular moral point of view, of our willingness to do something about an issue we consider evil or wrong, as our way of trying to make others do what we want them to do, as a sign that we are upstanding, righteous members of the community.

Our grief, sadness, sympathy, empathy, pain over another's misfortune are all signs that we truly care; the absence of such a show of feelings would be read by many as evidence of our coldness, lack of concern, love and so forth. Note, that the show of feelings does not have to be accompanied by any actual action, such as a real intervention of your time and energy. Most of these displays are simply cosmetic, the social lubricant that oils the ongoing transactions of our interpersonal network and allows us to be readily recognized as partners in the emotional mythology of a particular cultural matrix.

Thus, this third question, which amounts to, in another form, WOULD IT MEAN ANYTHING ABOUT YOU IF YOU WERE NOT UNHAPPY ABOUT THIS? This is really cutting to the heart of the assumptive architecture of beliefs; for here we are faced with the conscious acknowledgement that were we not to be unhappy, we would be seeing ourselves as cold, uncaring, unloving, immoral, strange, or indeed, quite mad! Here, with this question, comes the opportunity to know that we are using our unhappiness as a social tool to negotiate our way through our culture. Here, also, at some point in the process, do we come to a watershed decision. Once we begin to know that we do not have to be unhappy, unless we decide that we must be in order to avoid the opprobrium of society, then as we shed our unhappiness we come to see that eventually we will be nullifying the whole concept of evil. We will be seeing it as simply an assumption about reality that has its roots in our having lost touch with the absolute nature of our own self-creation when it comes to thoughts/beliefs/ feelings. Since we are literally the author of ourselves (*svayambhu* or "self-born in Sanskrit), the concept of evil becomes an extraneous myth that fades with the ever growing light of our knowing that there is no mystery to human behavior because it springs directly from our beliefs. That there are no mysterious forces afoot inside our heads keeping us from bliss. That we are the sole arbiters of our equanimity and that this is the great democracy of reality: that all have equal access to their happiness whenever they might come to admit its presence in their lives.

I Am Who I Am Who I Am...

"Nothing is either good nor bad but thinking makes it so." Shakespeare

Now we come to the threshold of our dialogue examples. We have seen in bare outline the nature of the dialogue as exemplified in the three basic questions. Let me say a word about my reasons for constructing these fictions of fictions as illustrations of the Option Method. Normally, one might expect a series of "actual" dialogues with clients that I have encountered, whose varied problems would highlight different aspects of how Option works in the life of individuals. I have written such a book, *Joywords: An Invitation to Happiness*, with nine detailed clinical instances and readers are invited to examine that work should their interests be for such an approach. Instead, here, I have chosen to utilize works of fiction and by altering them, create a tableaux of dialogues about the major issues of human life from an Option perspective. But, some might object, the author controls the dialogue, creates the arguments, sculpts the nuances, decides when a character is going to undergo a *metanoia*, that is, a transformation, or a change of mind. These characters respond just the way the author wants them to until it is time to draw all the threads of the dialogue together in a positive (from the author's perspective) conclusion. YES, EXACTLY!

I would respond that what is reflected in those fictions is the actual, essential rhythm of human life. We do create ourselves; we are writing ourselves out into the future through each living instant of our lives. We are our own characters living out the scripts of our beliefs in our own life "novels," as it were. Like the author of a novel, we bear the same relationship to our characters; they are our fictions, created for a multitude of purposes. There are no mysteries in the novel that the author has not created, none that the author therefore cannot solve by changing the script. Tragic endings or happy endings, or middles or beginnings for that matter. That is all in our hands:

A simple view of a person that is essential to the Option Method attitude is that each person creates and shapes (using his given body, i.e., all genetically inherited physical attributes) his own, individual personality in all its aspects, and apparent complexities, by means of the beliefs he chooses to accept as true; about himself, about other people, about the nature of the world and God, and especially about the belief in evil.6

The tradition of seeing art and literature as a sourcebook for a genuine examination and illustration of human behavior is not original. Sigmund Freud often made reference to the classics and told his students that no better example of human conflicts existed than in the works of Dostoevsky, the *Underground Man* in particular. Thus, in that spirit, do I claim that the examples to follow are as "clinical" as any standard clinical recounting, including my own in the aforementioned work I have written. For, what unfolds in each fiction is a self creating its own fictions and yet not knowing this! It is the knowing of this, that breaks the trance of created unknowingness. We create our destiny through the central truth of our own freedom that ultimately defines our own system of beliefs, borrowed to be sure from others and encouraged by innumerable layers of socio-cultural apriorisms. It is the making explicit of our role as the architects of our own destiny that releases us to surrender our unhappiness and to admit the truth of our happiness, should we so choose.

Chapter Two

Storming Heaven: the Myth of a Wrongful Beginning

Prometheus Bound!

As noted in our book's introduction, so much of human history is enmeshed in the experience of trying to find, the right formula, incantation, ritual etc., that would placate the wrath of an "angry god" (angry, presumably at our errors and mistakes) or somehow correct the errors of the age, the primal conditions that have set humans up in the condition of imperfection commonly known as "evil."

In all cultures, in one form or another, there is a "myth of a wrongful beginning." In the West, particularly in the Judeo/Christian/Islamic matrix, and its "secular" variants inspired by a host of philosophical perspectives, i.e. revolutionary Marxism, resting upon Hegelian philosophy etc., this concept of a wrongful beginning reigns supreme. A Messiah, either as an individual, such as Christ, or a messianic group, such as the "leading edge of the revolutionary proletariat," is required to enter into history and "fix" what is wrong or to create or restore things to the way they "ought to be." So whether it be Prometheus storming heaven for a share in divine prerogatives, or some other religious, ideological or scientific construct, humans seem always to be looking outside themselves for a *deus ex machina* to save the day and to bring the elusive religious, ideological or scientific millennium into being.

What is true in a broad cultural sense is of course true in the case of each human individual who is living out of the logic of some belief system and is plugged into a web of assumptions shared by others in the cultural context, so that certain kinds of responses seem "automatic." In this chapter we will explore this myth and some of the attendant beliefs that are relevant to everyday life. The vehicle for this exploration will be a rather exotic one. It will be a chapter, albeit my own version, inspired by a book written by Daniel Quinn, entitled *Ishmael*.

The aim of that author in writing his novel was to demonstrate that human beings were basically doing fine in their thousands of years of existence prior to what historians describe as the age of agriculture, which began four to six thousand years before the birth of Christ. His thesis is that humans were part of nature and lived in accord with nature, in a more or less balanced and harmonious way. However, with the end of the nomadic period, when groups took to agriculture and established permanent centers, a new interpretation of reality entered into the ethos of human tillers of the soil. This new vision gradually fell out of synchronization with the rhythms of nature and increasingly relied instead upon the myths of technology, with the goals becoming, not a harmony with nature, but the subduing and controlling of the environment and the subordination of all animate and inanimate realms to human desires. The root of this drive the author finds in the myth of human superiority, which he sees as a kind of derivative of the desire to be as gods and not to be subject to the laws of the universe. Thus humans, who had once considered themselves as partners in the world of life, now devised a myth of power to "storm heaven" as it were in a Promethean act of hubris. Since that time, then, using human capabilities to manipulate the environment through technology, we have created havoc among ourselves and our environment and are, in Mr. Quinn's opinion, on the way to a technological, environmental apocalypse. The fictional device he uses to illustrate this is a gorilla, named Ishmael, who somehow becomes a *sapiens sapiens*, a knowing knower, equipped with human intelligence and an ability to communicate telepathically. The reader is invited to enjoy Mr. Quinn's book to find out how all of this comes about. Our point, is that Ishmael acquires a human student, to whom he hopes to teach the truths of "how things got to be the way they are," in the hope that this human will be inspired to share this information with others and thereby, perhaps, change the course of human history back to a balance with nature.

We enter the novel at the very end, when things have taken a decided turn for the worse as far as the material fortunes of Ishmael are concerned. He had depended for protection on a benefactor who befriended him early on in the novel and who provided him with the means to live independently and to follow his mission to seek out a human that would become a pupil of a new, enlightened way to look at the environment and the evolution of life. Having lost his protector and benefactor, he ends up caged in a carnival, sick and dying. What I have done is to introduce yet a second gorilla, Job, with the same miraculous telepathic intelligence to provide an Option perspective on the myth of a wrongful beginning. Note, that the narrative "I" in the story is that of the human student who had studied with Ishmael. The "Taker" culture is the term Mr. Quinn uses to describe the mindset of humans after the agricultural revolution, as noted above, with its new imperial vision of humankind's role in the universe. The "Leaver" culture, refers to the mindset of humans prior to the advent of agriculture, again as described earlier, with a sense of balance and harmony with the world around. Let me underscore that this historical schema is not one that I personally ascribe to. But it does have elements of truth, as I understand it, sufficient to act as a background for an Option discussion of this myth and the clarification of some thorny basic issues such as the concept of "evil," as I hope the character of Job and his perspective will make clear.

Job's Response to Ishmael

Having arrived at the carnival, and having arranged to spend the time with Ishmael, through the usual procedure of bribing the keeper, I sat down in front of the cage. Ishmael was silent, and then acknowledged me with a raised eyebrow. Obviously, he was out of sorts, but something else was present. Without any further thought or reflection, I launched head-long into my questions: "I know that you said we had completed the learning in our last talk, but I have not yet been able to arrange your transport, and there are still some lingering questions, particularly in response to your description of the Taker culture as a prison and of your saying that it is the minds of people that must change; presumably each individual must undergo a mind change."

Ishmael showed no surprise at my presence or questions and bestirred himself but little as he answered: "It is perhaps some sort of appropriate destiny that you should return with these questions, for there is something new that you should know, something that is in some ways as startling to me as I am sure it may be to you. Another voice has arisen."

"Another voice?" I queried in return.

"Yes, another voice," and with that he inclined his head slightly to the right and my eyes followed the inclination to discover what had not been apparent to me before, perhaps because of my intense focus on Ishmael and the work to be done. There, juxtaposed at a kind of right angle to Ishmael's cage was yet another cage, about the same size. In the dim light, I could perceive a form, smaller than Ishmael's to be sure, yet unmistakably that of a primate, resting in the darkness against the back of the cage. Allowing myself to focus into that darkness, I was able to make out a face, leathery, more wizened, with eyes that, like Ishmael's, reflected a knowing that gave me to understand that they knew, really KNEW just as I knew.

"Job" came the thought, in a fashion I had learned was the same process utilized by Ishmael," my name is Job."

Silence reigned for what seemed like some minutes, but I am sure lasted no more than seconds in real clock time. "Job," I answered, as my head swiveled, or rather oscillated slowly from the shadowy outline to my left to the familiar hulking figure to my right.

"Well", came Ishmael's familiar intonation of thought (and indeed it was instantly clear that thoughts had their own distinct intonations, just as sounds), "it seems you are to be blessed with more than one teacher, with more than one perspective."

"But, how…" my voiced trailed off even as the new patterns of the dark form called Job interrupted gently, but with obvious urgency: "*How* would require more time than we may have," said he." And I believe if there is any contribution I can make to what according to Ishmael has already been a remarkable journey for you, then it will be best to forge on into our dialogue without delay."

I looked at Ishmael whose head nodded majestically in silent approval, as he said: "I must tell you that there are points of divergence and I myself have come to discover much in this most fortunate misfortune of our mutual discovery, Job's and mine. If I understand Job's position correctly, and he will explain it himself to be sure, we are in general agreement as to the flow of the history of humankind and the creation of a myth of dominance and necessity. This myth is based on the notion that humans sought liberation from the gods and sought the prerogative of gods to bind and dispense all reality as they saw fit, believing that this was their right and destiny to which all else on earth was subordinate. It is on the tantalizing point of the 'tree of the knowledge of good and evil' that the central character of our divergence takes place."

Job's thoughts symphonically blended in: "Yes, you have correctly identified the crux of the matter as it pertains to humans, but, also, interestingly enough, dear Ishmael, to us as well, since we perhaps are the only two primates other than humankind to attain to the status of *sapiens sapiens*. We, too, face what is unprecedented except in those who are knowing knowers, that is, the issue of happiness." "Happiness," I chimed in reflexively, "in what way is happiness at the heart of the matter we have discussed up to this point."

"Indeed," came the now clearly more Wagnerian tonalities of Ishmael's thoughts, "ever since we discovered each other some days ago, all our energies have gone into this exploration, and while I remain unconvinced finally, yet there is a dimension here that I had not reflected upon until Job brought it to my attention."

In counterpoint to the heavier melodies of Ishmael, now came the unmistakable complexities of what can only be termed Bach-like patterns: "Perhaps I might lay out my vision as I have come to know it over these many decades since I have attained the state of knowingness you call self reflective consciousness."

Job went on: "First, something that seemed utterly obvious once I came to understand it for myself. Though like Ishmael, I too spent little actual time in what you have identified as the "wild," there was enough time to know that equanimity, in the sense of being at one with oneself and the world was not an issue. The flow of our lives as animals was, as Ishmael earlier described it, like that of one finger on a large hand of many fingers. There was no unhappiness, but rather varying states of comfort or discomfort, of tranquility or of alarm, depending upon the collective mood of the troop. But the idea of being "unhappy" only became an issue when I came to the realization precisely that by knowing ourselves, we know the individual status of our being-in-the-world. We then know we are mortal creatures, we are aware of our vulnerable status as individuals and we have concerns not only about our survival, but more, about the very meaning of our existence. I understood how the notion of control, meaning control of our external environment, had become a ruling passion for humans. Indeed, as Ishmael pointed out, it is at the heart of the Taker cultural myth.

Yet, for our brethren in the "wild" as you have understood from Ishmael, there is no struggle for "control." The gazelle and the lion are prey and predator but for an instant; once that transaction of survival is satisfied, there is no anxiety in the gazelles who graze on the plains and there is no anger and hatred in the heart of the lion. The gods have set it up so that some will feed on others, not out of the passion for control, but out of the inborn instinct to survive. No more is reaped on the plains but what is essential to life. And where such sustenance does not exist, then there is death, not anticipated with existential dread and terror, but taken as a natural outcome of the flow of what is at any given time."

"So far so good, chimed in Ishmael." I nodded in agreement as well. Job continued: "So then, even among the early humans, and here we have scant information to form solid opinions on, but even among them, their life rhythms reflected the reality of the world around them. To take what was available, to kill game, to grow food even, but always to be in balance with the environment. Balance, not domination was the mode of being. Then we come to the "Garden of Paradise" myth, the apparent foundering point for your Taker forbearers, all revolving around the loss of a certain kind of innocence. Now let me ask you, "he said addressing me, "what was the property that Adam and Even lost in that garden."

"Just as you said," I replied," they lost balance with the world around them."

"Yes to be sure, but what was the essential feature of that balance?"

I thought for a moment and replied: "Well, as I discovered with Ishmael, humans traded the balance they possessed for the power in the knowledge of good and evil that they thought would make them as gods and put them in control of that very environment they had previously lived in balance with."

"Yes, precisely" said Job," But, still, you haven't identified the nature of that balance."

I sat in silence. My thoughts and gaze wandered over to Ishmael, who immediately through his blinking eyes gave me to understand that I was on my own. More, perhaps, it seemed that he himself was engaged in deep concentration upon what Job was elaborating.

"Perhaps it would help if I ask you this way. This balance that humankind had achieved was in concert with all the rest of life, was it not."

I nodded in assent.

"And the main feature of the balance as we understand it in animals is their equanimity within that balance. They 'neither sow nor reap' to paraphrase a biblical statement, and yet they have no anxiety about the past or the future, because for them there is only the immediate present and whatever may be required to deal with that present as it rises up to be dealt with. Is that correct?"

"Yes" I replied.

"Then, what might that imply for the inner state of humans, at least as represented in the primal myth of the emergence of humankind, even if the reality of human life eons ago might have been something different? After all, following Ishmael's outline, we are trying to understand how 'things got to be the way that they are' and why the Taker story is being enacted in the way that it is."

"Well," I began hesitatingly, "it seems that there is a parallel between the inner equanimity found in non-human life and the state of being humans identify with in the primal myth."

"Excellent" piped up Job. "Your pupil is worthy indeed, Ishmael."

Ishmael merely grunted without even intoning an eighth note of a thought. Job forged on: "Now, of course, that inner equanimity was alive, at least in the myth, in creatures who were different in the ways we described earlier, were they not. That is, they were not simply moved by instinct to follow a particular flow in concert with the program of the gods, but rather, humans actually could KNOW they were doing what they were doing, and so presented a qualitatively different manner of responding to themselves and their surroundings. What was that capability?"

"Well, they could and did know, as you said, that they possessed a past and could anticipate a future."

"Yes, yes, but what deeper reality underlies that ability to know a past and a future?"

"I suppose," said I in a voice filled with puzzlement," that they had feelings about what they knew."

"Feelings," replied Job with a slightly raised tone as if closing in on something important, "what do you mean by 'feelings?'"

"I mean they looked around and took in what was going on and had feelings about what they saw."

"So, said Job, "the looking around and the feelings are a related activity are they not?"

"How so?" I asked.

"That is, that the ability to perceive and to feel are inextricably linked; indeed they are just different aspects of the same reality. What is that underlying reality?"

A pause, a feeling of being stuck rose up within me, much as I had experienced when conversing with Ishmael many weeks ago. "Well, they had opinions about the world," I started in great hesitation, "and they felt deeply about the opinions they had."

"Close, yes very close" came the reply, "but let us fine tune the understanding. If humans are looking around, forming opinions about what they perceive and having feelings based on those perceptions, then might not an overall umbrella word like 'belief' describe what humans are forming and structuring themselves by? After all, what is a myth if not a belief that somehow reflects the collective belief structuring that has been going on in a community for some time. You learned from Ishmael that the human community, the 'Leavers' as he describes them, were actually the ones who formulated this myth of equanimity as a response, in some ways, to the encroachment of the Takers with their ideologies of control and domination. And that central to the myth was the moment when the primal human couple ate of the tree of the knowledge of good and evil; it was at that point that they lost their equanimity was it not? Logic would tell us that if they were just fine, in balance, to use Ishmael's term, prior to this knowledge, so what did knowing about 'good and evil' gain for them?"

Puzzlement was etched upon my face and I came to notice what seemed like a matching refrain upon Ishmael's countenance as well. We were poised on the cusp of some understanding, but what did Job have in mind?

"It was not what they actually gained, but what they thought they gained that is the point," suddenly interposed the heretofore silent Ishmael. "I have been at pains to get this one open minded human to understand that the vehicle for salvation that the human Taker society created out of their promethean act in stealing control from the gods is an illusion, a chimera. I have previously likened it to the occupants of a machine that is supposed to fly, and as the machine falls from a cliff, those within can temporarily point to the fact that they are, however temporarily, airborne. But, within a few seconds (read millennia for the Takers) they will know without doubt that their flying machine simply does not possess the capability to fly! They have taken this precipitous flight for success, even as they head straight for destruction."

"Yes, it is so," began Job in a slow deliberate tone with an especially respectful resonance directed toward the suddenly activated Ishmael, "human societies, with all their variants of culture, are basically still rooted in the mythological decision represented in that choice to know good and evil. Thus, then the importance of understanding the implications of that choice."

"Again," he continued," if equanimity was what was lost, and a convenient umbrella word for all the various forms of equanimity might be 'happiness,' then is it clear that the choice to know good and evil did NOT bring HAPPINESS. In other words, what the Leaver myth of the primal human couple is portraying is a situation in which the NATURAL state of being human is happiness! It stands to reason, then that what they actually did choose by 'eating the fruit' was UNHAPPINESS.

Now here you and I, Ishmael do diverge, at least as I understand how you described your story to your pupil. You spoke of the gods as the dispensers of 'good and evil' as if there were such an objective thing 'out there' that the 'gods' controlled. Surely in the kingdom of all life, such terms were irrelevant When God or the 'gods' created the earth and all the creatures upon it, he/she (they) unequivocally pronounced it GOOD. Unconditional approval was given to all that there was. So, later, as the Taker mythology takes over from the Leaver version, then good, evil, judgements, punishments and the whole paraphernalia of the polarity of good and evil become the rhythm of the Taker mentality. Humans are not only heading over the cliff to destruction in their illusory flying machine, they are aiming exactly there by reason of the inner dialectic created by a belief in good and evil, a duality whose conflict they contrive to resolve and master in endless ways. But in order to resolve this conflict, they would have to take a metaphorical trip back to the original assumptive choice point in the garden when they chose to leave the natural state of being happy and acquire what they thought the gods knew. However, the gods never knew anything about this at all, 'this' being the illusory knowledge of what is called good and evil. Let me tell the story more formally in the way that I understand it and perhaps that will clarify this even further.

The Myth of the Garden of Knowing: Unde Malum/ from Whence Cometh Evil?

Once upon a time, when there was "only" God, God decided to create all that there is and is coming into being. When done, or better when God had gotten as far as God wanted to for the moment, God declared ALL "to be good." Among the creatures created by God was humankind in the persons first of Adam and Eve. Initially they knew what God knew i.e., that ALL was good. But God endowed Adam and Eve with the total freedom to be whatever they wanted to be, to define themselves as they wished. In the garden of Eden, where they resided, they were perfectly at ease and in balance with themselves and with all around them. God did not direct them to know anything but what they decided to come to know. However, God knew that there were ways of knowing that would resonate with the essential understanding of what God and the universe were about and there were ways that did not. These ways that did not God described as "As If" ways. For God, *knowing* was *being*; whatever God knew simply WAS! That was how it was for God and God put the essential tone of truth about that in the resonance that was the song of the universe as it unfolded.

For humans, however, things were slightly different. Like God they were knowing knowers; not only did they know things, but they knew that they knew things. But not only could they know, but they could also "think" that they knew something, even if what they thought they knew wasn't a *something* at all! That was what God called "as if" knowledge, as mentioned above. So what God knew *was*. What humans knew could sometimes be or *not* be, depending upon whether it really resonated with the essential tonality of what was. Of course God knew all because God was all and God was having fun just unfolding and discovering God's own self and playing with that knowledge to create even more fun things to come to be.

Humans were tiny holographic reflections of God; that is they partook of the primary feature of God, the ability to create themselves. What they lacked, since they were still creatures, was the knowledge of all that there was. That could be God's alone. The joyful part for humans was in the open ended process of creating themselves, as the ages stretched out before them in the beckoning potential of what could come to be.

Now, in that garden, there were many trees with an infinite variety of fruits, or to put it another way, there were many things that humans could come to know in creating themselves. There were things that were real, in the sense that they really were, in the same way that God really was. Then there were all those things that were "as if" things, fruits of illusion and delusion. God wanted Adam and Eve to be like God in their joy of self-creation. But freedom is freedom, and they had to mold themselves out of the clay of each moment in ways that they saw fit. God did mention that there was one tree whose fruit would yield them nothing, the tree called "the knowledge of good and evil." Adam and Eve considered this advice, but were free to act in accord with what they thought best, and that was just fine with God.

Of course, you are all in suspense as to what happened. Yes, that's right, they ate the "apple." From this, they decided that they had come to know something momentous. What was that thing? It was that there was such a thing as evil. This thing called evil, they decided, was a force that like a sort of virus, was all over the place; it could be in other people, or things in the environment. Worst of all, it could cause bad or, what they now came to call, "evil" things to happen to and in people.

Needless to say, this discovery was very disturbing. When they brought this new information to God, God was silent. After all, it was their discovery and it was for them to do with it what they would. They took God's silence as a rebuke, as a sign that God was displeased with them. Wow! This thing called evil had now gotten them in trouble with God. New and extraordinary feelings began to arise in them. For one thing they felt a thing they called "shame." Roughly translated, it meant the state of feeling unhappy about just being who they were. They took God's silence as a proof that evil could cause terrible things to happen to them; further, that because these "terrible things" were happening to them, it must mean that there was something wrong with them! They fled from the garden because they didn't want to inflict their shameful presence on God.

One thing led to another; no longer trusting in their own ability to be in balance with themselves and nature, they acted out of a thing called fear. What this seemed to mean was that they were in a state whereby the anticipation of some terrible thing that was alleged to be going to happen in the future would be something that they would become miserable about and tortured by right now in the present. The more they were afraid, the worse things seemed to get. These were hard times. They grew to fear one another, because one never knew when this thing called evil, in all the many variants, would "take over" another person and that person would then do them harm. There were so many things to avoid: evil places, evil people, evil animals, evil thoughts, evil spirits. Particular individuals were designated in the burgeoning groups of human called tribes, to keep track of and to devise ways of dealing with all the growing evils that multiplied from generation to generation; they were called by various names, shamans, priests, witchdoctors, witches, wizards, psychotherapists, psychiatrists etc." Job paused for a while in order to allow the strains of the story to be absorbed by the minds of his two companions.

Quiet reigned for a few moments. Job's thoughts remained like the refrain of a symphony, ringing in the ears of the mind, notes that one would not easily relinquish. Job observed us both, giving time for replies if they were forthcoming. None were and so he continued: "Ishmael, you made much of how the murder of Abel, the keeper of the flocks and representative of what had theretofore been the 'balanced' way of human life, by Cain, the first representative of the 'Taker' vision of control and disharmony was a watershed act that adumbrated the end of the 'Leaver' story on earth."

"Yes, that's true enough," replied Ishmael in tones of confident confirmation," it was at that point that agriculture was subordinated to the goals of domination by the Takers"

"All right, then," elaborated Job, "I would like to embellish this with my own interpretation, since we are dealing with myths and myths are but the clay of human thinking and perceptions. It seems to me what is more important than the murder of Abel, is the fact that by that act it was Cain, the paradoxical champion of the Taker stance, who is marked forever. And note, he could not be marked from the perspective of the attitude of happiness found in the primordial garden. Because in there, prey and predator are not judged as 'good and evil' but rather just as entities engaged in the ongoing dance and rhythms of living and dying. No, in the garden 'all is approved of .'

Rather, the notion of guilt, fear, terror, miseries of whatever stamp, these are the fruits gained only through the knowledge of 'good and evil.' Cain represents the doom you talked of earlier Ishmael, but it is a doom because he had no choice but to be condemned by the new dispensation, the new gods of the Taker mythology. Cain created himself as evil, saw his deed as evil, did the deed out of the beliefs gleaned from 'good and evil'; from the derivative jealousies spawned by 'fear' of not having 'enough', though as you pointed out so often, Ishmael, 'enough' was never an issue for the Leaver residents of the garden. But for humankind and for Cain, the state of not having 'enough' was 'out there,' an objectivized 'evil'. Understand, that the core of obsession is precisely the exponential amplification of a perception based on fear. Thus the 'greater evil' becomes 'not having enough,' the lesser 'evil' becomes the domination/destruction of Abel, through whose death the state of not having 'enough' will be attenuated; thereby will 'evil' be defeated! Humans have acted out what they believe is a 'just morality' in its many cultural variants, based upon 'greater' and 'lesser evils', have they not?"

Ishmael nodded slightly and Job went on: "From such illusions of inequity and deficit come compensatory drives for power as the sole antidote to the inevitable existential terrors of being 'helpless' in a universe where a multiplicity of mysterious forces 'out there' are whirling in a malignant gyre that threatens to destroy your own desires for yourself in spite of yourself. This fear that the "I" is not adequate to maintain itself in the face of the 'out there' is also a core misperception."

"Yes" concurred Ishmael with what looked like a slight grin, "humans have always been plagued with the fear of demons, devils and soul stealers. I must admit, even among the Leaver cultures, there are 'voodoo' like beliefs that attribute the ability of witches or witchdoctors to literally cast spells and kill others by so doing. Those who believe in it do in fact die. I suppose you will take this as support for your thesis, eh Job?"

"It was your observation," twinkled back Job's reply.

"I guess the current version of that is the fear of aliens coming and abducting us and forcing us to do things against our will," I said joining the flow of the fugue." Would that not point in the direction of the same fear of loss of control over the self to some mysterious force 'out there'?"

"Bravo," shot back the sparkling thoughts of Job. "But what the gods know, and what perhaps a few humans have come to know, is that the 'I' is utterly integral to itself. There is no power anywhere, anytime that can in anyway make the 'I' other than it is or cause it to 'act against its will.' Why? Because it is in the very meaning of an 'I' that it is the supreme filter of meaning for itself. Alter that in any way, through physical destruction of the person or by some hypothetical cancellation of the physical substrate's ability to manifest the 'I,' and what you have is not 'I.' The very essence of self is the executive capacity not only to know itself but to DECIDE apart from any and all circumstances what it is going to believe, hence feel and express, about whatever is presented to it. We know from human history that no torture, physical or psychological can absolutely deprive given individuals of their executive capacity to decide how they are going to be with themselves. As long as the 'I' is present and able to manifest itself through its physical presence, it is able to decide its own fate, meaning the state of being of the 'in here' *Eigenwelt,* to borrow again a phrase from the existentialists. For the 'out there,' all is indeed contingency and uncertainty; but it is in the' in here' that humans live, breathe and truly have their being.

Yet for humans living out of this myth, the sole answer has been to 'take arms against a sea of troubles'; but, locked within the iron envelope of the logic of this myth, they can never 'end them.' Humans are forever driven by what they perceive to be the endless objectivized 'evils' and discontents that often seemingly magically assault them from all sides. Therefore, you must have 'more' of everything through the use of power and control: more of your own to populate and subdue the earth; more cultivated land and resource usage to support this fear driven population explosion; yet the more of your own you have manifesting variants of this myth, the more conflict you encounter as each 'Cain' tries to slay the current 'Abel' and preserve himself. To repeat, it is Cain then, who condemned himself to eternal exile from the ATTITUDE in the garden because of the acceptance of 'good and evil.' This is the true mark of Cain: not Abel's death, but his inability to have anything but hatred for himself in one form or another, no matter how it may seem not to be that, over having done the deed!"

"But what of forgiveness," I chimed in out of some irrepressible need to defend humankind, "even the Taker tradition speaks of and offers forgiveness, does it not?" The large form of Ishmael seemed to move in what I interpreted as a gesture of support.

"Ah," came the rejoinder from Job in dulcet tempo," and if you raise your voice to speak of human forgiveness, please save your effort. Forgiveness too is but an artifact of 'good and evil'; for, there is no talk of such a thing until the fruit of that tree is consumed, is there? Does the lion ask forgiveness of the gazelle; do other gazelles condemn the actions of the lion? True forgiveness is the knowledge that there is nothing to forgive!

Such forgiveness does not, and by the logic of the Taker belief structure, could not exist, precisely because it is the direct outgrowth of the attitude that reigned in the garden. You spoke truly when you said that the Takers in adopting that part of the myth could never understand it. The garden stands as an enigma to the evolution of the Taker story; for them it simply becomes just another event, another misfortune, the primal misfortune in an endless history of misfortunes: just another experience to be even more unhappy about!"

During this lengthy peroration, the figure in the cage, from whom these thoughts issued, barely moved. One could make out the briefest articulation of eyebrows and the change in the tonality of the eyes, with but little else to mark the passion with which the thoughts played in the concert hall of my mind. There was mind silence for a bit and when the music of thought began again it was Ishmael's cadences that flowed in:

"What are we to understand of your version of the human story then? As I have seen it, human kind has broken faith with life and out of its drive for domination is headed for apocalypse, carrying portions of the rest of earth's life, at the very least, along with it. What is imperative is that the myth that undergirds this promethean mania be deconstructed and that humans know that they are in the grip of a wrongheaded view of themselves and of their relationship with their environment. This is why I undertook to find a human who would come to know this and be moved to share the truth with others and they in turn with still others, until all could hopefully come out of this age-old trance and return to a balance with life." Ishmael ended with the strains of frustration and impatience trailing the communication. There were hints of depression coloring the edges of his "voice."

Job responded: "But my friend, are not you now by your attitude and demeanor in some ways echoing precisely what is at the root of the Taker myth?"

"How so?" queried Ishmael in a tone of weariness.

"Just so," came the reply. "Let me ask you in another way," continued Job, "if indeed you are unhappy about the way in which humans have enacted their myth/story, why are you unhappy?"

"Yes, it would be fair to say I am unhappy," said Ishmael. "Just look at the how things are and how they have come to be this way."

"What about the way things are and have come to be makes you unhappy?" asked Job.

"I have already shared that in some detail and so I shall not repeat it now."

"No, what I mean is why are you personally unhappy about the way things are?"

"Is it not self evident: because it is there to be unhappy about."

"What do you mean?"

"I mean the flow of history, the human atrocities, the rape of the land, the slaughter of countless species, the list grows by the second: these are all the ongoing tragedies that humankind is enacting out of this myth."

"Is that your way of saying that you don't want these things to happen?"

"How do you mean that?"

"I mean is not all your passion in whatever form, outrage, frustration, fear, hopelessness, is not all this your way of saying 'I don't want any of this, I never wanted it and I don't want it now.'"

"Well, yes, but these events, this activity, how could it not provoke one's unhappiness? To remain calm and unfeeling in the face of such apocalyptic prospects, it seems to me, would betray an attitude of uncaring and indifference, just at the time when the greatest concern is imperative if anything is to be changed!"

"So", continued Job in response, "are you saying that your unhappy passion is your way of letting yourself and the world know that you care deeply and want things to be different?"

"You mean is it my way of punctuating my concern so that others will know I really mean what I mean?" Ishmael paused and considered that a moment, and then replied: "Well, I suppose that is true in a way, but is not the expression of such feelings a natural accompaniment to one's perceptions about what one wants to be different?"

"There are two important points raised in your reply," said Job, "Let me take them one at a time. First, you said my observations about the use of your unhappy feelings were 'true in a way'. Let me ask you: in what way could they possibly be untrue?"

"What do you mean?"

"I mean, in what way could it possibly be other than true that your feelings are what you utilize to punctuate or accentuate the beliefs that you are articulating? I mean when you say 'a natural accompaniment to your perceptions,' are you not simply talking about what you believe to be true at any given time?"

"Well, yes, but I also mean that there are events about which one just has to be unhappy. It is in the nature of the event to draw forth the unhappy response."

"Are you speaking as an animal or as a primate that has acquired cognitive parity with homo sapiens sapiens?"

Ishmael considered this for an instant and replied: "I am speaking as both, since I have the advantage of knowing both states."

"From the perspective of an animal, then, where would your unhappiness come from? You have admitted that they live in the present. The lion and the gazelle do not live in anticipation of conflict or struggle with one another, do they? They meet the moment as it evolves and deal with it the best way they know how, is that not so? Indeed, your words, I believe, were that they accepted the ways in which the gods had set up nature, whether prey or predator, roles they found themselves in by dint of circumstances. Most importantly, that they 'were at peace' with that arrangement."

"That is true," replied Ishmael in a half mutter of the mind, "some of our brethren may border on self awareness, but the flow of their lives is indeed a present unburdened by the ghosts of the past or the shadows of the future. Let me say then, that in my role as a self knowing non-human primate, I share the human feature of being able to juxtapose the past with the present so as to understand the flow we call history; and, further, I am able to anticipate the future, and so plan for contingencies. I suppose, it is on this level that my 'unhappy passions' as you described them are relevant."

"Ah, and so," pressed on Job, "and so now you may begin to appreciate the existential situation of *homo sapiens sapiens*."

"How so?"

"Your argument with human kind, that is in its 'Taker' variant, is that they broke faith with life by trying to usurp the 'prerogative of the gods' and gain domination over the earth, that they could not accept what the other animals and presumably the Leavers could accept, and 'be at peace.' You further hypothesized, using the mythical frame of a conversation among the gods in the primal garden of paradise, that the gods themselves came to know equanimity in the reality that life and death among their creatures, prey and predator, were perfectly okay, that there was no requirement of guilt or unhappiness in any form about the fate of these creatures as they made their way through their existences; I believe you said, applying it even to the natural fate of Leaver individuals, that there was 'no shame' in death. The animals, at least, were 'at peace,' to repeat your phrase."

"I'm with you so far," nodded Ishmael.

"The problem for the gods, as you put it, "continued Job, "derived from the anticipation of how their premier creature, represented in Adam, would grow and blend with the rest of creation. It is as I described it in my telling of the garden myth. They wondered whether Adam and his progeny could handle the 'knowledge of good and evil,' the very knowledge that the gods themselves had come to a place of equanimity about. In other words, for the gods, the knowledge of 'good and evil' amounted to a nullification of the polarity itself, i.e., in essence there was only good or equanimity, else how could their creatures be 'at peace' with 'evil'? What they were doing, in actuality, was simply repeating the primal observation of the earliest "Leaver" version of God, who said that ALL was good. There was no 'evil.' It simply had no ontological status as a reality of any kind!

To repeat, then, their concern, those gods of yours, was over how Adam would possibly perceive the world if indeed HE were to eat of the tree of the knowledge of good and evil. Would he understand what they understood, that happiness, equanimity and acceptance was the key to the balance of all life with itself. Hence there would never be any need to control or dominate, since there was nothing that required such a posture. How could things possibly go awry? Would you care to speculate on this in the light of what I have said?"

Ishmael, in what seemed like a half smile, inclined in my direction, and queried: "I don't want you to feel out of the dialogue, so if you have any comments, they would be welcome."

"Indeed," piped in Job, "your vision is invited most heartily, since in point of fact, you are Adam for all intents and purposes and it is to you that your kind will listen. Our voices are not likely to survive, as your meeting us here in these surroundings gives good reason to indicate."

"It takes us back to what you, Job, earlier spoke of in regard to the primal myth of the first couple in the garden," I began, ignoring Job's allusions to his own and Ishmael's dire conditions for the moment, "that the 'natural' state of humankind was happiness and that what eating of the fruit gave was quite literally a knowledge of NOTHING. I say that in the light of your earlier comments and of what you now have asserted concerning what you term the illusory existence of the notion of 'evil'."

"Quite so, quite so," came Job's reply with a lilt of affirmation, "but knowing that this NOTHING has become *the* SOMETHING of human history is to understand the mythological engine that has driven and, now with ever greater intensity perhaps, does drive humankind to the brink of its own destruction. For," now turning to Ishmael again in direction of thought, "the rationale you gave in your explanation as to why humans placed such a premium on unending growth and control was precisely in order to have power over the SOMETHING that constantly threatened them, namely the force of evil that could somehow unseat them and force them to do things AGAINST THEIR WILL! This also speaks to your vision of human kind as living in a prison of their own making. Prison 'walls' keep the inmates in, but paradoxically, they also keep everything else out. That prison's first 'warden' was Cain who imprisoned himself to set the example for the rest of his fellows. This brings us back to the point that I began this dialogue with you, specifically, Ishmael. That is the point about the origins of what I called your 'passions of unhappiness' the felt experiences of what you believe about human destiny, and how you described them as created by forces 'out there' over which you had no control."

"You mean my feelings of dread and outrage over the way I see the Taker culture destroying the world" joined in Ishmael. "Yes, I did say that these responses felt 'organic' to the nature of the situation." "You said the situation evoked them," interpolated Job," and further, not to feel them would be unnatural. But you see, to return to the myth for a moment, the difference, again between the gods' perspective and that of Adam is that in the former case, the gods knew there was no such thing as evil, but Adam did not and took evil as a reality to be eternally dealt with. It was evil that humans were trying to avoid or control. And, since evil was an 'out there' phenomenon, resident in events and activities in the world, then the world became the logical object for human control and subordination. Only by controlling the 'out there' could the interior of Adam be secure. Thus was pseudo-causal attribution brought into being in the myth. Remember, in the classic biblical version, that when God asked Adam why he ate of the fruit, he blamed Eve, and when she was queried, she blamed it on the serpent. Thus 'the devil made me do it' was born, and inside that statement is the primal fear that requires humans to conquer the world. As described earlier the 'devil' or the force of evil, can make us do things 'against our will' and therefore, evil, the source of this intolerable state of affairs, which is a reified entity, must be conquered and destroyed so that equanimity can be achieved. Now you see, in my opinion, why the Taker myth was born, why it is being enacted, and how things came to be the way they are. Humans don't want to be destructive or life destroying. Everything they do, in all the cultural variants under whose banner they enact that myth, they are seeking happiness. However, because of the belief in the objective existence of evil, happiness can only be achieved by the TOTAL control of the world around, only by the TOTAL control of all the variables that humans throughout the flow of history have identified as the embodiment of evil. In one age it might have been the Leaver cultures because they refused to concur in the central vision of the Taker mentality (I hasten to add, that your version of the Leavers leaves much to be desired on this score, because they too bought into, with perhaps less dire consequences from the human historical perspective, the myth of the existence of evil. I would refer you the novel by Vargas Llosa, *The*

Storyteller, for a good example of this. In another age, evil might have been the Christians for the Romans, or the Moslems for the Christians and vice versa. More recently it has existed under the banner of the Jews for the Nazis, the capitalist exploiters for the communists, the communists for the 'capitalists' and so it goes on and on into apocalypse."

Ishmael rumbled slightly in his cage and gave forth with the barest pianissimo of a thought: "Yes, yes, that part is true." Job went on:

"For so long as the 'solution' to the human condition, as humans see it, rests with the control of the 'out there,' the *Um-welt* and the *Mitwelt* as the existentialists call it, there is no sense in bringing their attention to their self destructive course. They cannot do otherwise than they believe, as you yourself have stated, Ishmael; they must enact the story they believe in. We differ, as you can see, on what can be done about it. Thus, when I asked you why you were unhappy about human behavior, I was only pointing you in the direction of possibly seeing that in so far as YOU might see the world as 'evil,' as a place where the 'out there' ineluctably controls the 'in here' of your psyche, to that degree, then, do you yourself partake in the very Taker myth that you so fervently desire to deconstruct."

Job's cadences grew softer as he said: "You, as I, Ishmael, have gained much by our acquisition of the status of knowing knowers. But each of us must eat of the tree; each of us must make the critical decision about the basic nature of the universe. We can side with the gods, who in your own version of the story, (though to be fair you did not come to that conclusion precisely in this way) had to have decided that there was only 'all is good.' It was that that generated the basic ATTITUDE for all life that allows all to 'be in peace' to repeat your words. Or, as Adam and his progeny, and indeed perhaps as you yourself Ishmael, you can choose to accept evil and create endless reasons, following the logic described moments ago, to become unhappy in whatever form about the nature of the world. Whether the use of unhappiness will motivate self and others to do the 'right' thing or 'avoid' the wrong thing; whether through your righteous rage you will be moved to destroy what is 'evil'; whether through your despair you will 'create' guilt in others, i.e. somehow give them the unhappiness they deserve for not recognizing how they have 'caused' you unhappiness—the possible combinations within this iron envelope of beliefs is endless! For, in the pseudo-causal universe, rage engenders rage, Serb kills Bosnian who kills Serb who kills Bosnian ad infinitum."

The sound of my own voice ended the pause that ensued: "So, then are you saying that my acceptance of the direction of human history without judgement or rancor of any kind is somehow paradoxically the first step on the road to changing it?"

"You are deep in the neighborhood of truth in saying that," smiled Job. "I am not saying that you in any way have to like what has taken place. But it would be well to go further and understand that just as among the rest of animal life—when we live our life out as fully as we can in accord with that primordial Attitude that mythically reigned in the garden we are also by so doing living out this existence in fullest harmony with all our fellows in life. The resonance we create in such a manner is like unto a member of an orchestra providing the basic pitch for all the others. They can listen and accept or not accept the sound. In any event, it is for them to tune their own individual instruments in accordance with that resonance if they wish. When the community of individuals do so then there is the potential for symphonic creativity to occur. The critical contribution of the first member is to come to know for themselves the 'right' pitch, then to tune their own instrument, and only then to INVITE others to do the same.

Such an invitation is the highest form of compassion because it uncondictionally, nonjudgementally accepts that people are following out the logic of whatever they believe at any given time. Like the gazelle and the lion, they are 'at peace' even though they may devour one another! Humans have the added advantage, it seems to me, of achieving what our animal brethren cannot. As 'Leavers' they can leave off from 'devouring' each other altogether and find ways through their knowing knowingness, through the use of happiness derived, not fear driven, people-oriented technology, to give each other the space to live in utter harmony. Better yet, to be more congruent with trusting the spirit of freedom and uncertainty, let's let the Leavers do whatever the Leavers will do and let's see what happens!"

Now the tones of Job's thoughts achieved the most subtle pitch of what seemed an inner transport of ecstasy: "The exciting thing that I have come to know is that life is knowledge formed by the creative intelligence of the universe; the purpose of evolution is not adaptation (for if that were the case, life would have stopped at the bacteria who were as perfectly adapted to an environment as one can imagine). Rather we are drawn by what the mathematician Goedel formulated as the 'incompleteness theorem.' Nothing is complete, certain or static, nor is there any requirement that it be or ought to be so in any way, since everything is simply the way that it is and there is nothing to fix to make it alright! All is unfolding on the cusp of each instant, and we, the 'eyes and ears' of the process, at least in this corner of the universe, have front row seats at this unfolding; indeed, we are partners in the miracles of each moment's newness simply by our ability to understand that it is new! 'Strange attractors' of uncertainty and lawful unpredictability draw us forward, if we' have ears to hear and eyes to see' to quote your Bible again.

Thus, to paraphrase one of your forward looking Nobel laureates in physics, David Bohm, the universe through creative intelligence winds itself in infinitely varied whorls and gyres of ever increasing complexity, not because it is better, but simply because it is its joy to be the way that it is. Humans, as knowing knowers, have a place in this process if they want it; they can be 'stewards' of life on earth, as you described it, and be evolution's midwives as perhaps others like us, Ishmael, attain to that state of knowing knowingness; however, we (and I use 'we' in the sense of community with humans) also have the remarkable ability, precisely because we have FREEDOM, to believe and act 'as if' the presumed external entity called 'evil' stands in the way of what humans call 'fulfillment.' Here the meaning of illusion in its Latin origins as 'false play' takes on significance. In other words, the endless playful unfolding of what is (just watch animals playing in the 'wild') is a joy beyond measure. We who know have taken it to be otherwise because we CAN! So, even in our illusions, we confirm, paradoxically, the endless inventiveness of the universe in creating itself and in doing so freely—letting creation regulate itself as it comes to know itself. If humans let slip this golden opportunity—well then, so be it. The universe is doing just fine anyhow, thank you very much. And, while this may mean an ending for many of our animal brethren, they 'know' the flow of the universe through their balance with it, and, as you yourself said, there is no shame in death."

A great reprieve of brilliant intensity followed the break in Job's thoughts. For the first time, the form moved out from the darkened rear of the cage and shuffled laboriously over to the utmost corner nearest to Ishmael. Now, revealed in the dingy light was a creature in the veriest throes of decrepitude. An ape, probably a gorilla like Ishmael, but of such a mangy mien, as to be almost unreal, like a costume. Great patches of his body were bereft of hair; and wounds, scars and scabrous areas were everywhere apparent. It was obvious that one of his legs was either broken or paralyzed, because he dragged it along like a piece of wood beside him. He lodged himself at the point where the cages were but a foot apart, his breathing heavy and labored. I suppose he must have read my thoughts because he commented: "Does my appearance shock you?"

I fumbled for a reply and finally let out: "What I see would seem to affirm the ferocity with which the Taker myth has been enacted on you. I must admit, your appearance would seem to belie your philosophy as you have unfolded it here."

"How so?" came the reply.

"Well, it is beyond me at this moment how you can speak of accepting the Taker vision without rancor and at the same time to maintain equanimity, when you have obviously been treated with the utmost callous disregard for your status as a living creature and have been brought to this low estate, *in extremis* as it were; yet you maintain that you are happy!"

Despite the incredible weakness of his body, Job's thoughts arrived with piercing freshness and vitality: "My human friend, if you will allow me to address you as such, happiness is wherever you stand. At present, I am in a filthy cage, vermin ridden, and undoubtedly at death's door; but where else is there for me to be happy but wherever I am? Believe me, if you have some other place in mind for me to be to be happy, I would not be opposed to accompanying you forthwith."

Ishmael had been following the discourse with rapt attention, yet at the same time, it was clear how his body was also collapsing into illness. A wheezing sound accompanied his breathing as he reclined, one knee raised and his hand hanging weakly from the knee, with one finger tentatively raised. He turned to me and with tones both deep and gentle played out these thoughts: "You are the new Adam; you know all that we know and it is for you to decide its meaning and value as you see fit." A pause ensued and the thoughts returned at an even deeper register: "Our mutual journey is ended; yours now begins. Farewell."

With that, slowly, tremulously, Job's hand, pointer finger extended, moved through the bars of the cage and in an agonizing arc traveled the distance to meet the tentatively raised finger of Ishmael. Like the most resonant tones of a church organ Job's thoughts came through, as his eyes glittered with moist intensity of feeling: "All is good, dearest friend. Be at peace!"

With that vision frozen in my mind I leapt up spewing forth the words: "I will find a way to extricate both of you. First thing in the morning I will return with enough cash to buy your freedom. Hang on." I stood fixed for a moment. Neither Job nor Ishmael moved from their positions, nor did they acknowledge me any further. The time now was to act. All that could be said had been said. In an instant, I turned on my heels and sped out toward my rented van.

I shall not bore you with the circus of things that went wrong in my headlong efforts to locate enough money and all the ancillary events attendant to that. Suffice it to say, when I was able to get back, some days later, what I found were empty cages. The caretaker informed me, with the utmost look of condescension for the weak of mind, that the apes had died the night before last and that their carcasses had been hauled off to the incinerator.

I stood in the open space in front of the now empty cages stunned to the core. At first hot tears of rage and loss burned my cheeks even without reflection. When will it end, came the thoughts like needles in my mind and, for an instant, I could have sworn I heard a reply, 'when you are at peace.' I shook off the response and again attended to my grief, turning over and over in my mind my failures in not arranging a rescue in time of these two most precious and remarkable beings. As I turned to go, I tripped over the makeshift bench I had put together in front of the cages. Suddenly this lifeless conjugation of matter became the embodiment of all my anger. In an instant, I was kicking it into pieces, screaming at the top of my lungs words that I now cannot even recall, perhaps not even words but just the sounds of despair and outrage. It was only moments later when I caught sight out of the corner of my eye of the caretaker observing me with more than a little alarm, that I settled down and proceeded to walk away.

I say walk, but in fact I found it quite difficult to walk, because in my rage at inanimate matter, become animate for the sake of my rage, I had completely ignored my own body, whose legs, and particularly feet and shins, had been the instruments of my imaginary revenge on all Taker cultures. They were bloodied, bruised and throbbing with pain. While, pretending, lest the caretaker think more of the incident than I would wish, to walk naturally toward my car, I felt nausea rising up within. Again the refrain 'when you are at peace' came flowing into my awareness. Once within the sanctuary of my car I could both observe the extent of the self-inflicted damage more closely and also take some time to reflect on what had occurred.

"Wait", I said to myself, "does this not reflect what Job was saying. It is true, my love for these two extraordinary creatures was beyond my ability to understand; true, they had been casualties of all that they had revealed to me about my own kind and its beliefs about the world. But, what did I turn around and do in my 'natural' response to this 'outrage.' I 'murdered' a 'Taker' bench and in so doing caused MYSELF great damage. Am I not just repeating the process described by Job? By seeing what happened as 'evil,' I responded and acted on the 'out there' with great distress of emotion, and with great violence toward the 'out there evil' albeit 'only' a bench in this instance. True the bench is 'dead,' but what has been accomplished other than my own self-wounding. I let my breath grow easier within me, closed my eyes and allowed the resonances of memory to restore Job's voice. What if I were not unhappy about this; what if it were okay that this occurred. Would that mean that I 'didn't care,' as Ishmael feared?

After a pause, the answer came with the rhythms of my breathing: OF COURSE I CARE! The grief, the outrage, the 'murder of the bench,' what have they to do with caring. Do the gazelles get together a lynch mob to hunt down the lion? Again I found myself crying, but significantly different tears and feelings accompanied this flow. It was gratitude, I came to recognize in an instant. My God, to know that it is indeed alright, that 'all is good.' I felt the peace that I surmised must have been Job's and perhaps, in the last evening together, became Ishmael's. I even had a momentary thought to exit the car and 'restore' the bench, but the still vigilant figure of the caretaker in the distance instantly dissuaded me from such a restorative act. In any event, if gazelles and lions are okay with each other, surely the molecules in the wood that I had 'murdered' would understand as well. Besides, my legs were now growing so sore and stiff that if I didn't get back to my hotel room soon, I would be unable to drive the car.

I thought of the original advertisement that brought me to Ishmael: "Teacher seeks pupil. Must have an earnest desire to save the world. Apply in person." Hmmm, I thought, save the world. Well, perhaps 'save' is not the word, but rather, show how each person might affirm their own equanimity. I wonder what the world would look like were that to be the case? So perhaps I could say: "Teacher seeks pupil. All that is required is a desire to be happy. Apply in person." Yes, something like that. If I hurry I'll just have time to get it into the Sunday edition.

Primal Dread and Primal Awe: What We Could Know from Chapter One.

What is the essential question raised in this chapter? It is: *is there anything "wrong" with what is, with the way things have come to be?* We considered it from a global/historical perspective; that is, as Job described it, the vision of reality as flawed and requiring a collective human reparative response that organizes into myths of empire, utopias of every stamp, racial, economic, religious, power ideologies that purport to have the key to the mystery of the wrongful beginning and how to correct it.

What is offered in many forms is some path of attainment. It can be from a socio-political perspective, i.e., that all be part of some uniform belief system that may be universal or limited in its appeal, i.e., Christians, Muslims, Communists, Nazis etc. Additionally, a uniform code of ritual and interpersonal conduct may apply. From this matrix, it is implied, equanimity will come, either because some supernatural power will guarantee that the fruits of such deportment will be rewarded, or that nature itself is carrying out some invisible revolutionary program that rewards those who become its allies on the inevitable journey toward bliss.

Primal Dread "The Invisible Spheres Were Formed in Fright." Melville

From my perspective, such visions derive from what I call Primal Dread or Fear. This is, as earlier described, the vision of the world as imperfect, hence dangerous in a fundamental existential sense. Not only is one's physiological survival at stake, but more importantly, one's very meaning is at issue, one's very access to happiness.

Thus what all organized human groups endeavor to offer their adepts, in one form or another, is access to personal meaning, i.e., happiness. So, if we look within the communal program as the individuals attempt to apply it to themselves, we find them dealing with attempts to conform to belief patterns that will take them along a prescribed path of attainment to the achievement of equanimity. The models of achievement are many: the subtle mixture of opposites in the way of the Tao, the Buddha consciousness of the East, the life of the saint or holy person in either West or East, the exemplar of the totally correct acculturated citizen of totalist political systems, the perfect Nazi, Communist; and, of course, the adepts of countless splinter groupings organized under ever evolving and shifting popular patterns of belief, but usually involving some totalist schema and a guru-like living exemplar of that vision.

All, all of the above are based upon the premise of some version of the myth of a wrongful or insufficiently evolved beginning that generates the experience of the Unbearable Wrongness of Being. In contrast, I offer the vision of what I call Primal Awe. This is the experience of reality as being perfectly fine, that is, perfectly in accord with itself. There is nothing to fix, because there is nothing wrong or insufficiently evolved. Reality, the universe is simply the way that it is. Whatever changes occur within the framework of being are not changes from a wrongful or imperfect state to some better or more perfectly evolved state. They simply are the expressions of reality at any given instant of time as we experience it!

We are the ones who give shape to the universe with our appraisals of what is as being okay or in need of change. This we do from our individual vantage points as we engage each moment and decide what that means for us. Indeed, we may decide that some contexts are vastly more hospitable to our physiological comfort than others and we may discover endless ways to manipulate our environment on behalf of our own comfort and health. But this is not "fixing" an imperfect reality, so much as utilizing what is on our own behalf as we gain more information and apply that information with greater ingenuity and complexity. Thus, technology does not have to be derived, as mentioned earlier, from our fear driven needs to correct the unbearable wrongness of being in order to give us access to our equanimity.

From our primal awe of what is, we experience our happiness. There is nothing in life to turn away from in dread, fear, rage or disgust. What is uncertain is simply the freedom of the next instant beckoning to us to explore it to the full, if we allow it, if we are unburdened of the prisms of our belief that bend and distort the truth about reality into fantasied nighmarish forms and shapes that torture us and drive us to despair of our existences.

One young man I was helping can illustrate this further. Among his difficulties was a phenomenon known as a waking nightmare, or some would describe as a "psychosis." He would believe that ordinary objects could come "alive" as it were and take on a threatening aspect. Statues and pictures in his room could have this quality, particularly when he was alone in his room at night. After some months of working together and deconstructing myths of unhappiness in so many areas of his life, he came in with a remarkable story.

The previous morning, he woke up and as he stared directly above his bed, he saw a huge spider slowly descending upon him. At first he was gripped with raw panic and dread and was paralyzed at the sight of this creature moving toward him. Then, in the midst of this he stopped himself and asked what about this was so dreadful. Here was this creature, as big as a large dog, as real in sight, sound, smell even as anything he could know as real and yet when he paused from his dread and considered for an instant why he had to be in dread, two things occurred to him in a flash. One was that he did not absolutely have to be in dread, although it might be a good idea to remove himself from his bed immediately, but the other parallel thought was that such a thing as a giant spider does not actually exist. That's right, he said to himself, this is not real in any way, despite the fact that all my senses are telling me that it is. And, within that instant of knowing he shouted out NO THIS IS NOT REAL, I DO NOT BELIEVE THIS! Immediately the spider vanished; what was apparently real seconds before was gone without a trace. Needless to say, this experience only buttressed what this person had already come to know and had begun to live, that is, that we create our emotional reality and give it meaning. That spider was no more real than the many beliefs about the inevitability of unhappiness that my client had formerly believed to be the case in so many circumstances. Denying the spider ontological status was a crowning symbol of letting go of much unhappiness that had seemed equally as real only months before. The choice was to be in Primal Dread of this creation of unhappiness or to be in utter Awe of one's ability to shatter illusions and grasp the true fabric of reality, that is happiness.

Thus perception is the cornerstone that allows us to proceed with an ever greater admittance of our happiness, individualized to be what it is, to be what we experience it to be, to be an ever deepening realization of the truth of our own wonderment and awe about ourselves and the universe in the infinite and ever changing way we may come to perceive it.

So when we ask ourselves the first Option question of the triad of questions, WHAT AM I UNHAPPY ABOUT we could begin to know immediately as we inventory our experience that most of what comes to mind is something that is "wrong" and needs "fixing." This is not to say that there are not pragmatic problems in working out the everyday details of living. How to successfully acquire food, shelter, clothing and so on. We can and do apply ourselves to obtaining what we want in all those areas. It is, rather, when we say that things are not the way they "ought" to be or "should" be that our unhappiness arises out of the fear, the felt obligation, sometimes the obsession, to "make" things be the way they "ought" to be.

Chapter Three

Freedom, Guilt and Evil, the "Indispensable Minus": How Can I Be Happy in a Such a World as This?

The Brothers Karamazov of Dostoevsky: a Reprise of the Chapter "Pro And Contra" from an Option Perspective

Last chapter we looked into the myth of the wrongful beginning and the question of "how things got to be the way they are." In this chapter, we will broach the thorny issue of freedom, for this is at the core of the truth about happiness. As we describe our existences as contingent upon others or the world around us for our happiness, so do we unseat freedom from its central place in the history of any individual self.

Guilt is only a pseudo correlate to freedom. That is to say, we do not feel guilt because we are free and therefore responsible for what we are. Rather we feel guilt (that is bad about being who we are; shameful, and bad about whatever we have done or plan to do) because we believe WE HAVE TO! Not to feel bad about what we have done would confirm our basic evil nature and mire us more deeply, perhaps irretrievably into the morass of evil that lurks everywhere around us seeking to seduce us into ever more horrendous thoughts and behaviors. Now of course, all of this is governed by whatever cultural/religious/ideological rules that we have taken in and consented to as being valid for us. The proof that we believe them is precisely that we FEEL bad, or guilty or ashamed over having transgressed those rules.

All this pain and bad feeling is meant to be an internal corrective moral gyroscope, designed to give us a "shock" of moral pain in the form of guilt, etc., whenever we exceed the limits of the permitted. Presumably, this internalized pain device will maintain private and public order and promote the common good. Thus, does Dostoevsky call evil the "indispensable minus" in this novel, in the spirit of being the "necessary" contrast to the "good" that acts as a moral beacon to humans seeking equanimity. Of course, he is speaking somewhat ironically in his work, since the one who reminds him of this phrase is the avatar of evil, the devil himself (or herself, I suppose to be politically correct!).

What is important as preamble is simply to note the presence of "evil" and the apparent ease with which all fall prey to this reputed ever present malignant gravitational force drawing us to our moral doom. Seeing evil as present everywhere underscores why humans DREAD FREEDOM. For, with freedom comes the possibility of choosing evil, of being bad for ourselves. Better to contrive not to be free and thereby, perhaps escape the apparently horrible dilemma of being human:

People choose what they feel and think about anything People are free everywhere, and yet choose to believe that they are constrained in their opinions, beliefs, attitudes, decisions, and OPTIONS. WHY DO PEOPLE BELIEVE THUS? They choose to believe that they do not choose. In some way they must believe that they would be responsible for something bad if they had to realize that they freely choose. People fear being free because if they were free they would be 'too' free and would do evil or something bad.7

For those who are not familiar with the novel, what is essential to know is that one of the brothers, Ivan, understood as the intellectual or philosopher among them, is in a state of despair, tasting, as it were, *the unbearable wrongness of being* as all his assumptions about life seem false. Agitated and sensing a mental collapse he is haunted by what he perceives as the failed hopes of a utopian revolutionary youth and the further blows of unrequited love and the internecine struggle of his brothers among themselves and with their patriarchal father. We enter at this point in the novel with this version of what could have been. This hypothetical reworking would come after Ivan's long discussion with his brother Alyosha and after he has had an experience with another apparition, seen by him as the devil.

A Double Retells the Legend of the Grand Inquisitor

Ivan was sitting alone in his room, the conversation with his brother Alyosha, and the taunts of the petty demon still pulsating in his mind. His feelings were a mixture of incredible agitation and precipitous depression, as he stands on the edge of an abyss and shudders over the thought of how delightful it would be to just hurl himself headlong into it, to let go of all restraints and finally let happen whatever will.

Just at that instant, he thought he heard a voice, a familiar voice, indeed his own voice say: "Why are you so unhappy?"

Ivan froze and after a moment relaxed slightly and resumed his tragic ruminations, but then, again, he thought he noticed a shadow, no something more substantial, something nearly human, sitting in the chair across the room, hidden in the semidarkness created by the pale flickering light of the candle. He rubbed his eyes and blinked several times, but he could not shake the sense of a presence not eight feet from where he sat. The figure was motionless as if wanting a more formal invitation to be in being. Ivan's hair stood up in the back of his neck, but then, eyes glittering, he laughed in the fullness of despair and half shouted, half whispered:

"Yes, yes, this is the abyss. Why shouldn't I see the face of my own madness. Come, come into the light and proceed with whatever purposes move you to be who you are."

With that, the figure moved slowly at first, and then with gathering assurance, as if delighted with a newly experienced corporeality, until he was in fact sitting on the divan directly in front of Ivan. Now, even in the anemic light of the candle, Ivan could see the stranger in full figure, no not a stranger at all but himself, yes unmistakably him, perhaps a bit younger, but there he was, as if he had just boldly stepped out of a mirror and somehow was here, a willful, self created replica of Ivan. Silence ensued for a moment before Ivan broke in:

"Are you my final torment? The other apparition had the courtesy at least to be an "other" and not myself. Am I to suffer the ultimate humiliation of losing myself to another before I dash the cup and finish with the business of life altogether?"

"I may be a mere reflection of you," began the double slowly," but I am that half of the fullness of human possibilities that you just might want to listen to."

"Ha," spat back Ivan," you are a sorry specter indeed to be the mere reflection of one who is himself but a mere reflection and soon to be even less than mere. Away with you, I do not require the dubious consolation of your presence to confirm my misery."

"What are you miserable about?" queried the double in an even, neutral tone.

"What, well *what* indeed," smiled Ivan with barely restrained rage. "Where to start is more the question. Have you dropped from the moon? Oh yes, in a way I suppose you have. You are but the projection of my incipient madness made palpable by the condition of being on the borderline of fragmentation. Are you the lost innocence of my youth, the abandoned shell of idealism and the feverish fermentations of late adolescence?"

"I am what I am," replied the double calmly: "you recall moments years ago when you thought and wrote sentiments of joy and optimism about life and the world. I can be those potential moments and sentiments reborn for you, if you allow it."

"God," shouted Ivan as he brought his fist full down on the table in front of him, "are you going to throw those wretched imaginings of a hopelessly naive mind all too infected with the myths of what might be in my face? Spare me, for I shall rend you into the shadowy shreds that you most certainly are should you attempt that, I warn you!"

"Not at all, "came the reply reassuringly," I am simply offering you to know what in truth you already know but have merely forgotten. That is why I have asked you why are you unhappy?"

"So," started Ivan, sobering up slightly and scrunching up his face with curiosity, while leaning across the table in the direction of the divan, "you would know from me the roots of my misery, would you. Very well, though certainly you must know them already if you truly are what you purport to be. Nonetheless, why not. It will be nothing if not amusing in some ironic way to speak to myself in one finale, one crescendo of blistering deposition about the true nature of this accursed existence. Where to begin, for the litany of human sufferings and heaven's high crimes cram the dusty shelves of history. I am unhappy because the world is the way that it is, a world where fear, hate, greed, power, pain and destruction are the ruling virtues. Where evil rides the high horse and gleefully accepts praise and adulation from the ignorant, adoring multitudes, while the pious and the meek nurture their weak and bleeding bodies in countless dungeons, where women and babes cry to the silent heavens their endless complaints of rape and untimely death. That is but the briefest menu of the travesty of what passes for life in our age, perhaps in all ages."

"Then," came the reply in firm syllables, "what would you select from that menu as being the item that you are most unhappy about?"

"What about the cry of a child in the stillness of the night after its mother has been foully murdered. Yes, there is a juicy item worthy of note.

Tell me, my very self, what joy is to be found here? What happiness flows from the cries of that desolate waif?"

The double's reply came back quick as thought itself: "What about the situation you describe causes you personal distress?"

"All about it my dear, the stinging nuance of every change of tone of that baby's shrieks finds its painful resonance in my heart."

"I'm sure that is true, but still what specifically upsets you?"

"Merciful heavens is not the thing itself evidence enough of why I would be upset. There is death, desolation, abandonment and unrequited longing here. Surely you see these things even with your shadowy eyes!"

"Whatever I may see, what about this vision is so painful for you?"

"Ivan brought his fist down again on the table but then slumped slightly forward in a gesture of deep fatigue: "The thing itself, then, you would have the thing itself," started Ivan with a tone of abiding weariness, "well let it be that I reject it all, the whole awful sideshow of existence with all its false promises and broken vows. I say it plainly, there is something wrong with the very nature of what is! It is from that basic flaw that our multitudinous miseries derive and have their being."

"How do you mean that?"

"Just as I said it. It is a fraud, a kind of divine joke that we believe ourselves to be other than pawns in some evolving larger picture. Whatever the forces at work, they are of no relevance to us, puny bipeds."

"Do you recall your own earlier assessment of this vision, the story about the Grand Inquisitor?" "That poetic travesty. I warned you about dredging up the past, but then again in some sense I suppose you are my past, and perhaps my future too. In any event, you do me a disservice to remind me of having had those thoughts and worse of having actually brought them to life by writing them down. Must I endure the intellectual vomit of my former days now? But stay, no, perhaps there's pleasure, *à la Karamazov* even in that. No, go ahead, tell me to myself!"

"The tale I will tell is not exactly the same as the one you might recall, but by telling it this way, it may present you with a sense of options for understanding yourself and the world that presently are not what you experience and believe. Will you hear it then?"

"I said as much, did I not. Say it out as you choose. I'd as leave have my double rewrite my words as some fawning or pretentious editor or critic."

"Very well. As you know the story begins in Seville, in the 15th century, when the Cardinal Archbishop, the Grand Inquisitor, notices a commotion in the square while on his way back from the cathedral. It seems the populace were gathered around a figure, lean and Semitic, who had just resurrected a dead child as that child was being brought for burial. The crowd was awed and aroused by this extraordinary event and murmurings of praise began to rise up, when the wizened old man had the stranger arrested and brought to his private chambers.

Alone with the stranger, he addressed him "why have you come back? Your presence here the first time was disruptive enough, your promises were impossible to achieve; the masses only fell into despair over your teachings. We have corrected your work and given them the necessary excuses for their failures to be what you wanted them to be."

"What do you mean," came back the stranger's voice, deep and resonant.

"You know what I mean," replied the old man impatiently. "You spoke of love and joy in freedom and what has history taught us except the opposite; that there is only confusion and suffering in freedom."

"How do you mean that?"

"That freedom is an illusion since choosing is a disastrous activity for the majority. They torture themselves with what they should be choosing and how badly they feel for not choosing the right things." "What do you mean by 'choosing the right things'?"

"The things that you prescribed as the path to follow to salvation."

"Whatever you may have understood my message to have been, let me ask you this question, why are you angry about the way people use their freedom?"

"Because they don't know how to use it properly and only cause themselves grief and harm." "Even if some people claim to be unhappy by virtue of their not choosing the 'right' things, why does that upset you or anger you?"

"As I said, their freedom is for the development of right attitudes and sanctity, and they seek golden idols which we now happily provide them in various forms; by endowing humans with freedom you have only ensured their continuing unhappiness."

"In what way does freedom ensure unhappiness?"

"Because then they must believe that they are responsible for their actions and thereby suffer with guilt for their wrongful choices."

"Are you saying that you personally suffer from guilt because of what you call your 'wrongful choices?'"

"That is my purpose, don't you see. We have taken away the burden of freedom from the people and they have become as infants or sheep. We prescribe for them the total texture of their lives, but do so compassionately in the sense that while we demand strict obedience, we are quick to overlook many of the peccadilloes of human nature. We make it clear that they are not responsible for their actions, that they are but followers who must simply adhere to our merciful dictums and so avoid the pain of regret or guilt over how their lives proceed.

I have taken upon myself the burden of guilt in the knowledge of freedom and good and evil and will gladly bear the consequences of my creating for them the illusion of well being. Indeed, I am far more merciful than you precisely because I have opted to shield them from the glaring light of freedom, the horrible freedom to be miserable in pain and in want."

"What do you feel guilty about?"

"All the laws that are broken, all your commandments that are breached by the herd of hapless human sheep. I contrive to hide this from them but I cannot hide this from myself."

"What do you mean when you say 'laws'?"

"I mean the eternal verities that of course no one can possibly live up to, but nonetheless there they are to be obeyed or to suffer the pain of non-compliance. Only now I alone, along with some of the truly compassionate, suffer for them."

"What do you mean by 'eternal verities'?"

"Ha, this is truly a wonder. You are asking me! Well, of course there is the *mysterium iniquitatis* standing in the middle of history's path, the great spirit of evil which has stymied progress if we are to believe tradition. Evil is all around us, informs all of our instincts, debases all of our intentions, causes us to fall in spite of ourselves. Better to cooperate with the Great Spirit who offered you true wisdom in the desert; there is compassion in just letting oneself dissolve into the inevitable."

"What do you mean by 'evil'?"

"What indeed! Why, you who are the quintessence of unattainable good ask what is evil? Evil is thinking feeling and acting against what is good. Our fear of evil is perhaps primal, since it seems to corrupt the very process of choice and somehow, mysteriously, we end up thinking or feeling or acting a way that we did not want, against our wills as it were. Ah, and anticipating your question, then, what is the good? The good is right thinking feeling and acting."

"What do you mean when you say evil thoughts, feelings or acts or for that matter good thoughts, feelings or actions?"

"Curse you and your questions; this all harkens back to the beginning, to the baleful choice of our forbearers to forgo Eden; but they too could not bear the burden of goodness. What is goodness? Is it not ultimately what God approves of, even as Evil is that which God disapproves of?"

"What do you mean when you say 'God approves or disapproves'?"

"I mean that God decides something is good or evil."

"In what way does God decide that?"

"I do not know. God is free to choose as God pleases."

"Precisely, and did not God give to humans the same facility to choose as they see fit."

"Well, ostensibly God did indeed do that; but that divine trait of freedom is too intense for mere humans. That is why your message is in error, that is why we have corrected your work!"

"What do you mean when you say freedom is too intense for humans?"

"I mean exactly that they end up in the vast majority of cases choosing wrongly."

"What do you mean they 'choose wrongly'?"

"That they do not choose the things that they are supposed to choose."

"What do you mean when you say 'the things they are supposed to choose'?"

"I mean the things that would align them with the Divine Will, not things that involve their base instincts or selfish pursuits, though that is all humans are truly fit to follow."

"What do you mean when you say 'Divine Will'?"

"Well, that is what God wants and desires."

"Do you believe God wants anything else than happiness for humans?"

"Oh yes of course, but then in the same act of wanting happiness for them God endows them with that one divine attribute that guarantees it to be unattainable, that is freedom."

"Does not God act from God's knowing and is not what God knows what is?"

"Yes that is so."

"But do humans have omniscience in the manner of God?"

"No, that's the point, they fire their freedom blindly into the night not knowing what the purpose of their power is."

"If they are not omniscient, then they can only know whatever they know in the very moment that they know it and act, given all the circumstances that flow into the moment of their acting, is that not true?"

"Yes, I suppose that is correct."

"So they are always acting out of what they are believing is real or 'good' to use your term in the moment that they are indeed acting."

"That is true, but what they may be enacting may not be 'good' as we, as, I understand it."

"Yes, but it would be good as they understood it in that instant of action, is that not so?"

"Ah, but whose version of good is the good, if we all are seeking the good, does it not matter what we do?"

"Whose version would you prefer?"

"I am obliged to say God's, since God is the author of all Good."

"That being the case, then is it not written that at each stage of creation, God pronounced all that is 'Good'?"

"Yes, but how can we reconcile that divine appraisal with what has followed."

"What do you mean?"

"The horrors that have ensued as humans, yes humans alone, since nature acts without malign intent, humans have so scourged themselves with their freedom that all cannot be good. Has not even the divine complained about the conduct of humankind. There are many things that are written, after all."

"Many things have been attributed to the Father and to Me, that do not come from us. My question to you is if all are acting from what they know and believe in the moment they know and believe it, then how can they be held accountable for what they do not know and do not believe?"

"Ach, you bring questions that are truly worthy of the fire, the very fire that I personally often light under those who insist on their freedom."

"Does not the Church as it exists insist that no one forswear their own beliefs if that is what they truly believe, even though it be in direst contradiction to most sacred doctrine and highest authority. Are not those whom you burn often the bearers of greatest truth about freedom, that it is the most elevated of all human traits, indeed it is what the Father gave that makes humans to be human, the very essence of shared divinity and grace."

"So, then, is that your message now; that all are good and none are evil, indeed that evil is an illusion, for what could it mean if all are seeking the truth as they see it out of their freedom. But, most hateful damnation, I have personally been responsible for the painful deaths of many; I have borne the guilt of the herd and its sins are upon my shoulders. Am I a mere rogue or simply a fool?"

"Are you saying that you are unhappy about the specifics of your life?"

"I am maddeningly in despair, and have been so before your most ill timed return. You come again with the words of freedom and now I hear the words of compassion, that all are good but were I even to accept your teaching, what of those who have known the tortures of the fire?"

"What about your having killed these people is painful for you?"

"Their faces twisted in agony, their cries against me, against God, against their cursed fate; not all it is true, but many. How dare I allow myself to feel the felicity, the balm of happiness when these souls knew only perdition at my hands?"

"Are you saying that your way of making certain that you know that you care about what you have done is to bestow this intense pain of guilt and anguish upon yourself?"

"How could I do otherwise and remain sane. How could I still the screams that yet echo inside my mind and not feel that I would be even a worse monster than the multitudes already have named me to be."

"Are those screams and that pain, I repeat, then your way of making sure that you are not the monster you suspect yourself to be? And what are you afraid would happen if you were not to hear those screams or feel that pain?"

"Why then as I said," and the old man now twisted up in a posture of pleading and anguish, "I would truly be insane, beyond all hope of redemption."

"And when you carried out all these deeds for which you now suffer so fiercely, did you not believe at the time that they were the appropriate thing to do to preserve the Faith and order as you understood it?"

"Yes of course, but because of those beliefs scores have perished. It is true also that I have attempted to soften the burden, as I have understood it, of people's conscience by giving them permission to sin and call it something else, but still I carry the mark of slayer and torturer. I should not have been the agent of destruction."

"What do you mean when you say 'you should not'?"

"I ought to have done otherwise."

"But if you were doing exactly what you knew to do given your beliefs, then what could it mean to say 'I should or ought to have done otherwise.'?"

"Ach, again," grunted the Inquisitor uncomfortably, "you torture me with questions." He paused and put his bony and withered hands to his forehead in a gesture of solace and introspection: "So, it is true as I think of it now that I could not have done otherwise. Are you saying in essence what I have only partially said, and then only by way of believing that I was creating an illusion; that is, are you saying that *All is Permitted!* That there is no wrong, no evil, that people are always doing the best they know how given what they know and believe at any given time?"

"I am saying only that *All is!* Being requires no permission to be."

The old man slumped in a nearby chair with his hand outstretched upon an adjacent table. He paused for a moment. The stranger stood quietly and patiently by, then the old man spoke:

"Then can it be that my railing against freedom has all been a misunderstanding? For if I am to believe you, no, to say more accurately if I am now to believe myself, then humans have not squandered their freedom; they simply have been exercising it as they have seen fit, each according to their beliefs. And can it further be that I and others like myself over the centuries have aided and abetted the illusion that humans could not handle freedom and required some relief from the very thing that most makes them like unto God.

Indeed we have instituted three pillars of illusion to placate the masses, Miracle, Mystery and Authority. Miracle is the illusion of no self-sufficiency. It is the myth that to be is too painful without the promise of external transformation or magic to sustain hope, the myth of the necessity of an outside agency required for happiness since the hope of happiness through personal freedom is scant. Since we then believe we have no control over ourselves (that is after all the essence of evil, the experience of our loss of control and the terror and hopelessness it inspires) then, as I say, we revere what seems to offer us sustenance, that is, whatever force seems to get us some of what we want, or believe we need, particularly when we have experienced ourselves as impotent to get that for ourselves. It may be the *panem et circences*, the bread and circuses of political power or the mysteries of religion which gives us (at least as I have arranged it here) the aura of having received it under the auspices of the arcane, the unknowable. Thus they believe that their welfare is dependant upon us totally; that they are a mystery unto their very selves and as such require the exegesis, the interpretation of Authority, Hierarchy to explicate themselves to themselves. Secure with that interpretation, they might then have a modicum of the modest goods and pleasures we might deign to dole out to them as it seems politically astute to do so to maintain control. Further, from the promise of miracle comes the illusion of mystery. Mystery, again, is the assertion that life's burdens are bearable only through some unknowable schema which is revealed to the elite; through their exclusive possession of that knowledge, and their manipulation of that knowledge to foster the illusion that the populace is secure from the evil of loss of control, they, we, thereby gain the last leg of the Trinity of Power. They acquire Authority over the masses precisely because they are the fount of the yearned for miracles which are mediated by them alone through the arcane gyres of Mystery which thereby encircles the elite with the requisite mantle of Authority as the dispensers of this hidden wisdom. For to speak the truth, we have lived out of Dread, the Dread of Moses to see the face of God, the Dread of falling into the clutches of the Great Spirit of Evil through the enigmatic loss of control. We, I, have resented that Dread, but have attempted to shield ourselves and the people at large from the truth, as we understood it, by controlling freedom, lest in their freedom, they might offend the Dreaded God of Wrath. Even your *Euvangelion*, your 'good news' was not taken seriously, because the burden of Good and Evil had not been resolved, and as long as these concepts abided with us as realities, then freedom was truly a terrible risk; better the servitude of the confused and the bewildered than the dreaded solitary vacuum of the free."

"What do you feel now about that?"

With an almost vacant, wistful stare, lips pursed in a look of disbelief, the craggy figure examined something inside himself, then with a face that changed from disbelief to puzzlement, he exclaimed: "For an instant, a blessed instant, one that seemed in a way almost sweetly eternal, I felt so strangely unburdened, so light, so free in here," and he accompanied these words by pointing to his midsection. "Thoughts, even memories of a time when I would walk by the sea as a child and chase the seagulls, smell the soft excess of the sea wrack and turn into the wind with arms outstretched in the joy and vitality of a life just beginning, all this came instantly flooding into the space in here where only leaden, numbed sensations existed. Not since the earliest days can I recall such feelings. But then," and his brows clouded over with anguish, "the wall of darkness crowded in on me again and like a stone of unimaginable weight I found myself once more possessed of all the intensity of my pain, yea even yet reinforced somehow by my having dared to allow myself a respite from bearing the cursed garments of my shame."

"What about allowing yourself to feel a respite from your pain distresses you?"

"How dare I offer myself what I have withheld from others who have begged it from me."

"What about offering this to yourself do you find unacceptable?"

"How does a monster like myself deserve any respite?"

"What do you mean by 'monster'?"

"I despise myself for having been and being who I am."

"Are you saying that it would be wrong for you to be happy in the way you were for an instant just a moment ago?"

"The very stones of this city would cry out in protest against my delivering myself from this guilt."

"Are you saying that your guilt and all the distress it implies is what you need to make sure that you are not the monster that you claim you have been and are now but somehow would be in even worse fashion if not for the guilt?"

The old man's eyes flashed as he studied the stranger's face for a moment and then a barely detectable grin colored the edges of his mouth as he responded: "That does sound somewhat inane doesn't it. I have been what I have understood to be a monster over these many years, but, as I have come to understand from our earlier discourse, I have also been what I believed I was supposed to be, what I was acculturated to be and informed and accepted I should be, given what I did in fact believe. Even when I was out of faith with your teachings and attempted to correct your work, I was sincere, however I may have gnashed my teeth. My guilt, then, never helped me to be any different nor to deter me from my chosen path when I believed I had to act."

"Then, what would surrendering the guilt and its feelings mean about you?"

"What I traditionally have believed, although I never made it explicit, and only now see it in this light, is that the guilt somehow preserved me from being totally lost in my deeds. Yet, not once did it deter me, not once did it cause me to offer succor to those crying out from the flames. Indeed, in some strange way I cannot yet articulate, it often enraged me further, drove me on to even greater cruelties, as if I resented those who cried out for mercy as if *they* were causing *me* the pain of *my* guilt! Yes, time and again I overrode those feelings and would only feel the pain more intensely by way of compensation."

"And surrendering the guilt?"

The old man turned his face away from the stranger and as if speaking to the wall said in a bare whisper of astonishment: "I would run again as in my childhood on the beach with a body free of pain and full of zest and wonder." There was a long pause and suddenly the old man sprang from his seat and fell on his knees before the stranger, hands uplifted in a gesture of pleading; tears and sobs broke from his body as he shouted hoarsely to this still figure: "But how, how can this be! To feel felicity, happiness, joy in a life, lived so long in the darkness of misery and despair, a life obscene in its length because it shortened so many other lives. How can it be that happiness is mine? Can there possibly be another so undeserving of it as me?"

The figure remained still and gazed full into the agonized face of the sobbing old man: "To be is to be human and nothing that is human is alien to me as one of the Latin sages wrote *'Homo sum et nihil humanum a me alienum puto'* What do you mean, then, when you say 'deserve'?"

"Is nothing deserved then? Is all truly free? Are all equally invited to feast upon happiness as they find it through their freedom?"

"What about that being true do you find difficult?"

"Then not only was my avowed villainy, however sincere over a lifetime, in vain, but so was all my suffering about it!"

"Would you rather it not be true so that you might have your pain?"

The kneeling wizened figure grabbed at the stranger's hand and shook his head violently from side to side: "No, no, no," shot out his reply, in tones of rising assertiveness, "the words of your original teachings were to proclaim the joy of the good news about being. I felt so alienated from those words by virtue of my beliefs about freedom and what I considered its enigmatic, hateful consequences. Now the scales have fallen from my eyes and I am glimpsing what appears to be a whole new shape to reality."

"And how do you feel about that?"

"I feel like the archest of heretics, and yet I feel that there is hope after all. My soul had dried up with disgust over life and being and now rain has fallen upon the desert of my spirit. No longer do I feel obliged to defend what I never loved nor cherished; no longer do I feel obliged to sacrifice others on the pyres of illusion to buttress what is truly illusory: the existence of Evil and therefore the assumed untrustworthiness of freedom, the exercise of which would presumably only subject hapless humans to the risk of hopeless entanglements in the snares of Satan. Now I can find my former self, so long lost under these magisterial robes," and with that he stood up and tore off his dark princely outer garments and revealed the plain inner dress of a peasant, a commoner. "I have always worn the coarsest of clothing beneath the canonical dress of authority; it was my way of proclaiming secret solidarity with those that I brutalized, though for them it was the emptiest of gestures. Now in this very dress, I will leave this place, this sepulchre of the smoldering ashes of miracle, mystery and authority, and I will live what time remains to me in the coastal land of my childhood. To others I will leave the defense of illusion. Perhaps some day your teachings will find fertile soil among the tribes of your creatures. The trappings of my life up to now I cast aside, not in judgement, but with the deepest true sense of compassion I have ever known. For ALL are happy even in their not knowing. The mercy of the truth about being is that *ALL IS!* Not in the sense of being permitted, but simply in the sense of being, being freely, spontaneously in all the ways that being has and will manifest itself."

Now, still gently holding on to the stranger's hand, the somewhat less stooped figure of the old man, eyes glittering with gentle tears, spoke softly: "My deepest gratitude to you dearest teacher. Tell me, where do you go now?"

"I follow the will of the Father and the wisdom of the Spirit. And I say to you, the life of the child that I returned to its mother is a miracle pale by comparison to the miracle of your freely coming to know the truth of being through your own freedom. Go in peace." And with that he stepped forward, embraced the ascetic body of the old man and planted a kiss on his cheek. Then, he turned and in a flash was gone. After a moment's pause, the old man too, after the briefest glance around him, exited the door and was lost in the anonymity of nearby street crowds...

The flickering light of the candle on Ivan's table wavered as the double ended the tale. Ivan, silent and transfixed, sat frozen in a posture of total attention and it seemed like ages before the silence was broken. Ivan's tongue felt thick and unwilling as he struggled to speak:

"The man-god,"came from him in twisted guttural tones barely comprehensible, "the man-god is what you have regurgitated to me, that folly of my arrogant youth. All is lawful indeed! The Christ of my story was silent and you have made Him into a Socratic stooge for your own purposes. Do you wish to dispense with Evil when another apparition earlier aptly described Evil as *the indispensable minus?* I threw my tea at him in a gesture of contempt, but at least he knew the truth about morality. What, would you have me overstep the barriers of all the old morality, as I spoke about it in my stupid statements of years ago? Shall I plant the flag of the man-god, even if it be a solitary flag [For who shall dare to ascribe to such notions], in the middle of the human community and proclaim 'All is Permitted, All is Lawful,' at least for me since nothing is forbidden to God? Shall I declare a feast of happiness joy and unending love without the trials of earthly woe, without the teaching constraints of morality, without the threats of pain and damnation, without the promises of heavenly bliss eternal in a life beyond life? Shall I decree this life, however configured and acted upon in freedom, to be sufficient warrant for happiness in the moment, whatever the moment may bring; for love without debt or obligations, need or reward, no matter what the response or lack of it? *C'est charmant* as the other apparition would say; he is the one who said that the idea of God must be smashed so that the new order might be proclaimed:

As soon as men have all of them denied God…the old conception of the universe will fall of itself…and, what's more, the old morality, and everything will begin anew. Men will unite to take from life all it can give, but only for joy and happiness in the present world. Men will be lifted up with a spirit of divine Titanic pride and the man-god will appear. From hour to hour extending his conquest of nature infinitely by his will and his science, man will feel such lofty joy from hour to hour in doing it that it will make up for all his old dreams of the joys of heaven. Every one will know that he is mortal and will accept death proudly and serenely like a god.... (F. Dostoevsky, Brothers Karamazov, Grosset & Dunlap, N.Y.)

Ivan paused, and with a fierce glint of defiance in his glowing eyes, his jaw set, he stared intensely at the double. The other did not move so much as an inch, remained with a calm, benign look on his face and at last said: "Would you have preferred the Inquisitor to have continued in his pain and guilt and thereby continued in his unloved and uncherished but undoubtedly ongoing work of burning heretics and, since we are quoting ourselves, what about your version of the Inquisitor. Recall his admonition to Christ about the illusory nature of freedom and the necessity, therefore of submission:

Didst thou forget that man prefers peace, and even death, to freedom of choice in the knowledge of good and evil? Nothing is more seductive for man than his freedom of conscience, but nothing is a greater cause of suffering...Thou didst desire man's free love, that he might follow Thee freely...In place of the rigid ancient law man must hereafter with free heart decide for himself what is good and what is evil, having only Thy image before him as his guide. But didst Thou not know that he would at last reject even Thy image and Thy truth, if he is weighed down with the fearful burden of free choice?...But with us all will be happy and will no more rebel nor destroy one another as under Thy freedom. Oh, we shall persuade them that they will only become free when they renounce their freedom to us and submit to us.... And all shall be happy, all the millions of creatures except the hundred thousand who rule over them....who have taken upon themselves the curse of the knowledge of good and evil. (Dostoevsky, Grosset & Dunlap, N.Y.)

The double continued: "And so I ask you again, would you have preferred the Inquisitor to continue with his 'corrected' version of Christ's work?"

Ivan turned his face away from the double, half snorting his answer: "No of course not, but is the choice then really between the terrible freedom in the knowledge of good and evil or soporific submission to the blind collectivity of an 'anthill' utopia?"

"In what way is freedom 'terrible'?"

"Ah, I know, I know. I heard the tale you wove about how the old man's coming to know that Evil is an illusion based on some fundamental Dread that being is somehow flawed at the root and hence requires some constant correction and eternal vigilance against the forces spawned by that flaw. That Evil then somehow blunts the purposes of freedom and causes us to feel and do things against our will, the 'primal terror' I believe he called it. But is this not the foolish petty demon of mediocrity prancing and fawning before us, promising us that we can be happy simply upon our own decision to surrender our unhappiness. Suppose we are wrong?"

"What do you mean?"

"I mean what if we are mistaken?"

"What do you mean by mistaken?"

"Damn you specter, know you not the language and its meanings? I mean who or what has promised us that we are going to be correct in all our choices and particularly if we choose this overarching choice to cut loose all our present woes and the beliefs that presumably create them?"

"In what way could you possibly be wrong?"

"Ah, so you are going to repeat the dialogue with the old man about all doing the best they know how given what they believe, is that it?"

"Is that what you understand from my questions?"

"Can it be true that happiness is all there is and we are unfolding the universe to ourselves in the best way we know how according to our choices, given what we believe and know in any given moment?"

"What do you believe?"

Ivan turned to the double full face, grabbing the front of the table with both hands firmly gripped and leaned almost pleadingly in his direction, saying with a great force of words bursting from his breast: "Specter, I do so yearn for what you describe to be true. But can happiness be bought so cheaply, without the agonies of struggle and doubt. How many countless generations have come and gone, living in the throes of endless variations of myths and illusions that brought them precious little succor, at least as it seems to me. To simply reach out, as it were, and grasp fully the chalice of felicity and quench the endless thirst of human suffering by a change of perspective. Well…it is either the most audacious villainy or the most compassionate revelation; it totters on the borderline of genius or madness, I am not sure which."

"What about believing this troubles you?"

"I cannot, I dare not surrender this maddening doubt, this torturous worm of fear gnawing like a thousand insects at my very being."

"What are you afraid what happen if you were to surrender this torturous worm of fear, as you describe it?"

Ivan paused, still poised in viselike tension, gripping the edges of the table till his knuckles turned milky white: "My God, if I were to give up this doubt and fear, then I would be helpless before my own freedom, before the possibility of my own happiness."

"Are you saying that your way of ensuring that you do not place yourself in the position to make such a choice is by creating so much agony of doubt and fear that you would never accede to such a possibility?"

Ivan's glittering eyes turned vacant for an instant; his whole body frozen in the posture of holding on with fiercest intensity seemed to shudder in its maximum effort. Then, the shuddering ceased and ever so slowly, accompanied by an extraordinarily long exhalation, the body relented, the grip relaxed and he shifted gracefully back into the chair until he was stretched out along its length. Then he spoke: "So, I struggle against what I most yearn for. This is truly a marvel in the Karamazov tradition. I was the one who taunted Alyosha, my dearest brother, with the tales of tortured children, the little girl locked in the outhouse with excrement smeared on her face, the tiny boy forced to run naked while dogs tore him limb from limb in front of his mother, all to satisfy the pique of a general's wounded pride. These tales were designed to ensure that he, I, would never relent in our endless agonies about the horrors of life. That happiness would remain a taunting, devilish dream, and for that reason I threatened to dash the cup of existence to the ground, to return my very 'ticket' of being back to God and spit in God's face in defiance of such a world where things of this nature could occur."

"In what way has God anything to do with the things you describe?"

"Oh no, I understand. God simply gave us freedom and the ability to be happy, to be standing in the awe of being and to be filled with its unending joy. Now I see that it is we who are the creators of illusion. Out of our fears, doubts, agonies, jealousies, hatreds, rages, we have created the face of the human landscape. And, no matter how it looks, it has all been done believing that it was the thing to do. The parents of that little girl, the angry general, they were all acting out of their version of an unhappy world. Yet, over and over again we stand righteously in defense of the very mores and beliefs that inspire such actions. Then, we wring our hands in the throes of disbelief that the world could possibly be so harsh and cruel. Perhaps we, they, are all Karamazovs at heart. Well," and now he stood up full length and made as if he were going to move toward the double, "now is the time when this Karamazov steps out of the circle of illusion and into the light." And with that he moved toward the double who also stood up as if in anticipation of Ivan's intentions. But, as Ivan went to throw his arms around him, he found himself embracing the empty air. Brought up short by this, he stood dazed and then he heard, (it was clear but seemed more in his own head than in the open space in front of him), unmistakably his own voice saying: "And now you have yourself to yourself whole and entire. What you now embrace is not the empty air but rather the *you*, the very self that you have at last discovered. You have no need of me for now our voices are as one!"

The Cursed Questions

In the Russian intellectual and literary tradition of the 19th century, the term "the cursed questions" referred to the basic questions about life and its meaning. In this chapter, the Option questions have been highlighted and their import, hopefully, amplified in the dialogue between the characters. As you review these questions in your own mind: WHAT ARE YOU UNHAPPY ABOUT?, WHAT ABOUT THAT MAKES YOU UNHAPPY?, AND WHAT ARE YOU AFRAID WOULD HAPPEN (WHAT ARE YOU AFRAID IT WOULD MEAN) IF YOU WERE NOT UNHAPPY?, you can perhaps pick up the rhythm of the process between the characters in the story.

Here the primary issue was one of freedom and guilt, but what could you know in reviewing your own life that reflects those themes? So many times people have come to me with these concerns. One woman recently came filled with anxiety and panic over being in a relationship she no longer wished to be in. However, her parents believed that it would be wrong to leave the relationship, that it would go against the moral imperatives they believed were to be observed at all costs. The actual way in which the procedure unfolds, unique to the manner that each person opens themselves up to acknowledging their beliefs, is what resolves their unhappy feelings. In this person's case, the question, "What do you think it would mean about you were you not to be unhappy about the disapproval of others?" proved to be a crucial, transformative one for her. Truly knowing this, she soon deconstructed the major structure of her belief in her unhappiness, and joy and peace were the accompanying legacy of that decision. Take a good look inside and allow your creative impulses to see how you have written the script of your own life production.

Chapter Four

The Painful Passions of Medea

Perspectives on Love, Hate, Betrayal and Victimization

In this chapter we will endeavor to expose some of the most widespread mythologies of unhappiness about human relationships. All that has been described up to this point can be of great aid to the reader in comprehending the apparent paradoxes that love and hate represent. How can intense feelings, affection, joy in being together all disintegrate and transmogrify into frothing hatred that can eventuate in the most extreme acts of violence? In this version of the classic, we will explore these questions and conundrums.

Although composed centuries ago, the complaints of Medea about her role as a female, her victimization by men, the constant sense of impending and actual betrayal of women by men, all of these themes echo down the ages and have become the banner of what are now called "women's perspectives." In this rewrite of the play by Euripides, the interlocutor with Medea will be a female head of the chorus. The story line is simple and contemporary in the sense of the aforementioned age old themes of the "war" between the sexes.

Medea's husband, Jason, whom she aided to retrieve the Golden Fleece according to legend, lives now in exile because of reversals of fortune, despite Medea's desperate interventions. Now in Corinth, he has decided to marry the daughter of the king, Creon, and establish himself in the halls of power in this adopted land. The story opens with Medea vowing vengeance of the most extreme kind, i.e., the murder of her own children as well as of Jason's fiance and father, because of her rage over her perceived grievous use at Jason's hands. It is in the midst of this tumult that the dialogue begins:

Medea

Cursed is my fate for having loved so base and false a man as Jason. Through all the travail of his days, I have helped him to secure his rightful place. When my ministrations suited his purpose, he attended to me as his true wife, friend and lover; but now, when fate has proved false to us and we face the cold and icy hand of exile, now he turns to another to feed the fires of his ambition. This he does despite my steadfast devotion and our loving sons, the double fruit of our wedlock.

Chorus Leader(a woman)

What about his actions merit your displeasure so deeply?

Medea

His betrayal wounds me to the quick. Men use us and discard us as it pleases them to do. A woman's lot is one of suffering and chance.

Leader

In what way is that so for you?

Medea

It is not just true for me, but for many. I am now just one more example in an endless line of wronged women, whose lineage stretches back into the forgotten mists of time. As for me, the thought of his discarding me is more than I can bear.

Leader

In what way?

Medea

Did I not serve him well? Were not my wiles as cunning and fair as any others? Did not the service of my bed provide him with manifold pleasures to equal the arts of any other? He wanted for nothing. Did I not turn my back on beloved family, nay betray the very fountain of my own being out of loyalty to him? What plots, intrigues, even murders were hatched and executed from this mind and by these hands on his behalf. All to fall like ripe fruit to the ground after a storm, there to rot in hateful obscurity.

Leader

Are you saying you did not want to do what you did on his behalf?

Medea

Yes of course I wished it! My passion was in furious flower. There is nothing that would have turned me from my purpose to possess him utterly for my own.

Leader

In what way did you or do you now possess him?

Medea

Now, oh now he is lost to me, winnowed out of my embrace by his own greedy ambition and wanton lust. Before, he was fully my own, flesh of my flesh, one body and heart beating in rhythms of erotic rhapsody and common purpose.

Leader

So, then, he was with you when he wished to be with you and he has left you when he wished to do so?

Medea

All this is evident and true.

Leader

Then in what way did you ever possess him?

Medea

Your question runs its course to some purpose perhaps. A woman is a fool who thinks she has ever more than a precarious hold on any man.

Leader

What do you mean?

Medea

As your question implies, my possession of Jason was an illusion. All my wiles were for naught, since they fall like fledgling swallows against the stormy might of his caprice.

Leader

And how do you feel about that?

Medea

There is a boiling sea of rage inside of me sufficient to have sunk the fateful ship from Argos with all its valiant crew, the very ship that brought him to me. May Jason perish in his infamy and may I be the instrument of his perdition. All shall I take from him, his bride, his ambitious hopes, and even his loving sons, the useless treasures of our now moribund bond.

Leader

What about his treatment of you so enrages you?

Medea

What, is there not enough in his conduct to merit rage? Why, the very trees would set their limbs against him were they to know what I know, feel what I feel. Does he think that there are no consequences to shunting me aside. Am I some bauble thrown up by the sea to be admired, a temporary instrument of adornment, and then thrown back? No, he will feel the sting of my revenge, or these woman's breasts never gave nurturance to his manly brood.

Leader

Even though he has abandoned you, still what do you mean when you say he has 'merited' your rage?

Medea

Why, is not the merit in the deed itself? For loyalty, loyalty is returned, for love, love, but for treachery, treachery many times over does he merit. My treacherous deeds on Jason's behalf brought death to my father and grief to my sisters. Alas, blind is love in its inception and brutal in its morality. My deeds issued forth from my passion. All the more am I

resolved to crush Jason because of the legacy of treachery I left behind me
on many a shore on his behalf.

Leader

Still, how is the merit in the deed itself?

Medea

Why the deed feeds the fires of our perception. We see, yea feel the tres-
pass of others against our interests and our passions body forth in defense
and anger. 'Tis like a spark to driest tinder that engenders flame.

Leader

Are you saying then that it is the fires of our individual perception that
determine our specific passions?

Medea

As so it would seem, but the deed, the act, the circumstance may press
so dearly against our perceptions that they cannot but respond in kind.

Leader

Do we then choose how we feel or no about what life presents to us?

Medea

When the deed usurps the bonds of what can be borne, then we are
helpless before the deed.

Leader

Then what of Jason? Has he not offered similar reasonings to explain
his change of passion, that is, the extremity of life in exile and the require-
ments to secure for him and his sons a noble future?

Medea

Speak not of his reasons lest my rage spill over to touch thee. His villainy is secure in his freely choosing to abandon me and to seek his own
separate destiny.

Leader

So Jason's actions flow from his free choice; his passions' change are the
fruit of knowledge and volition. Wherefore, then, are yours exception to
this understanding?

Medea

I know not how they are but they are!

Leader

Is that what you truly believe?

Medea

Damn your questions! So, let be that I, like Jason, choose my passions. If he be damned by his, so let me be damned by mine. I will not be turned from my purpose in this matter.

Leader

In what way are you "damned by your passions?"

Medea

I feel the fire of them in my belly, the searing pain of his rejection. This is a wound that must be requited.

Leader

What do you mean?

Medea

I mean that I cannot, I dare not let him have his way in this affair.

Leader

What about his "having his way" would be so painful for you?

Medea

It would mean that he would live the sweet life, enjoy the newness of a virgin's charms, garner the wreathes of glory at Creon's court, spawn new offspring to warm his age and watch his present children grow in nobility and prosperity. While I, wretched and alone seek the uncertain hospitality of unknown lands, bereft of husbandly comforts and the balm of children's love. No, he shall never taste the nectar of life while I drain the dregs of vinegar and ashes.

Leader

Even were Jason to prosper in the manner you predict, what about that would prevent you from seeking your own felicity?

Medea

How could I possibly experience any felicity when the memory of what was and what might have been would be burning in my soul, tormenting me through endless days and nights?

Leader

Why do you believe you would have to live tormented by your past and present?

Medea

What else remains for me if not the path of suffering? At least if my vengeful inspirations carry the day and Jason suffers this great fall, then my solitariness will not have the torture of the wild imaginings over Jason's good fortune.

Leader

Be that as it may, in what way would your actual fate be any different whether Jason prospers or loses all. Will you not still be alone and in the self same condition that you lament so deeply?

Medea

It is a fate already prepared for me; I cannot escape it, do what I will.

Leader

So, then, if Jason has decided for his own reasons to follow the path he has chosen, in what way will your vengeance alter that decision?

Medea

My vengeance will alter nothing; it will only give me the solace of the painful companionship of Jason's loss.

Leader

What do you mean?

Medea

It is as I explained before, I would not have it that Jason prosper while I languish.

Leader

What do you mean by "languish?"

Medea

It is as I have described, I would be alone and friendless.

What about being alone and without friends distresses you?

Medea

You share the same sex with me. Would you desire such a fate and would it bring felicity to you?

Leader

I would respond to such events however I might; still what are your reasons for being unhappy about such possibilities?

Medea

I know not else, then, what to answer to such a question.

Leader

Would it mean anything about you were you not to be distressed about such a fate should it befall you?

Medea

Great gods? Would I then be breathing? Would life still remain in this body, already made frail by pining and woe? Not to be the viper's handmaiden in such a circumstance as this were like to being lifeless, some thing inanimate and not a true feeling and loving woman whose genuine devotion was so cruelly trod upon by a selfish man.

Leader

Are you saying that without your rage, your plans for vengeance and all the attendant miseries and fears, you would not know that you are a woman of true worth, nor that you greatly dislike what Jason has chosen to do in your regard?

Medea

In truth of course I know those things without my painful passions. But, wait, not to feel this rage, why that would be to bless the twisted course of Jason's logic. I will not stand abject and naked in acceptance of his will. Oh what a fool, the object of mirthful scorn I should be were I to accede in meekness to this man's shameful conspiracies.

Leader

Again, are you saying that without the pain of your distress to prompt you, you would not know your displeasure over Jason's course, nor offer yourself what solutions you might discover to turn your fate to the truest directions you find possible?

Medea

Foolish woman, your endless questions begin to sap my resolve. Ought there not to be consequences when men neglect their vows or dishonor us with their wanton ways?

Leader

Whatever consequences you might devise, still, why do you believe you have to be unhappy, enraged or in pain about what Jason might decide to do?

Medea

Because it is only the fire of my rage that fuels the resolve of such dire consequences as I conceive, the death of foes and beloved sons alike. Without that fury I truly fear that all should slip from my grasp and I would be the butt of all men's laughter to fulfill the age old vision of woman's weak and spineless nature.

Leader

Are you saying that such consequences as you have devised require your unhappiness in the form of your rage and pain to carry them to fruition?

Medea

'Tis true. I have no appetite without my anger to lay a murderous hand upon my own issue. And though I would rather Jason remained faithful to me, I do not truly wish the death of Creon or his daughter, if the fires of my purpose are not fed by pain. Other ways I might devise to bring to Jason's ken the outcomes of his actions, but not through so dread a deed as this.

Leader

And how do you feel about that?

Medea

There is a lull within me, but I know not whether it be mere surrender or the portent of another sense of myself. Another pain appears when all the rage, if but for a moment, vanishes. It is the pain of wonder and doubt. Why did Jason abandon me for another, even if it be for worthy reasons of state and to secure a better fate for our children?

Leader

What do you mean?

Medea

What do I lack, what art or arcane knowledge is absent from my being that could not hold this man to my bosom?

Leader

Why do you believe it means anything about you that he chose what he chose?

Medea

Surely, if I possessed charms and wiles in greater abundance he would have stayed the course by my side. Oh, what a grievous fate to be a woman and to be chained to the uncertainties of men's steadfastness made inevitably worse by the unavoidable decay of beauty as time makes its claims upon our hapless bodies.

Leader

Are you saying that with whatever charms you might hypothetically muster, you would have it within your power to make Jason love you if that were not his desire?

Medea

Well, I cannot pretend that I could bend his will against his own advice. That, I believe, we settled earlier when we spoke of his freely choosing what he would; indeed it was for that reason that I hated him, that is, that he chose someone else, for I do not believe he was somehow put upon against his own best judgement. Were that not the case, I would not have been able to hate him, for without his free choice, what would there have been to take issue with? Why would I rail against Jason, and not the fates, were his decisions not decisions, but the mere reflection of the blind forces of the universe that would move him and all as mere pawns in a game beyond our knowing?

Leader

That being the case, then, do you still believe that your lack is the occasion for Jason's decisions?

Medea

Wondrous to say, there is a new feeling in my bosom, though I know not how long it will linger. The cauldron that has brewed the broth of hateful anger and vengeance is calmed. While it is still most deeply my desire that my life retain its former lineaments, still, if is not possible, I know I can forge a fate that suits my talents. Was it not I who found ways to defeat the dreaded beast at Argos, was I not the one whose subtle diplomacies smoothed Jason's path, and was I not the one whose steely resolve removed all obstacles without flinching? The lore of woman's weakness is but myth and folly. I shall not further contribute to it by surrendering my inner peace on the altar of my rage. I'll make what place I can here, or seek horizons that will learn to welcome and appreciate my presence. Farewell sweet friend. Thy questions do credit to thine own womanly strength.

If You Really Loved Me You Would...

The very nature of love is at issue in this dialogue, and through it we can see so many myths exposed. But first and foremost, there is the myth of "owing" love to anyone for anything. Is not the very quality that Medea yearns for in Jason his FREELY gifted love of her? What she immediately appeals to as evidence of his treachery and betrayal is how he has turned to someone else, after she had so intensely given of herself to him and the cause of his advancement.

Here, we are seeing the myth of "earning someone's love" exposed to view. Do we earn anyone's love? How does a child, just born, "earn" the love of its parents? Should they withhold their love until the child can "earn" it? Love, charity, is a characteristic of the person who loves and derives from the Greek *xaris* which means freely given; it is "a gift of freedom for the one who possesses it." Another characteristic of love is its spontaneity, again a word which in Latin *sponte*, means offered of one's own accord, offered without any apriori agenda or purpose or gain in mind.

So, freedom is the primary matrix that generates love. What is free is by definition not bound or owed or obligated in any way. Getting back to the play, Medea's anguish is over her belief that love is an obligation, something owed. Yet, paradoxically, as noted above, what everyone truly wishes is that love be precisely what it can only be if it is to be experienced without anxiety or fear: completely unconditioned by obligation or oughtness in any way!

Now, if love is a gift, a quality of the possessor of that love that belongs utterly to that person and can in no way be encumbered by anyone's claim to it, then, it follows, that while no one has a claim on our love, so also do we have absolutely no claim on another's love. However, as we can see from the pain of Medea, her vision of love is highly conditioned, burdened with myths of obligation and demands of every sort.

The sentence that would capture her version of love is "You should love me BECAUSE…." There is no because in love, precisely because love is causeless in the most fundamental sense of being the spontaneous, that is freely willed, expression of a self towards another not in any way necessarily because of what someone has done for you, or even in spite of what someone may have done TO YOU! LOVE IS LIKE REALITY ITSELF, HAPPINESS ITSELF, IT SIMPLY IS! That is whenever it is, it is unpredictable and ineffable and completely locked in the hearts of the selves that alone will decide to create this gift or not. Cultures, religions and ideologies may try to engineer it or generate it by rules, dictums, imperatives of every kind as part of the belief architecture of that system, but, in the end, it eludes all attempts to create it outside the awe filled and autonomous reality of the self.

Thus the oft repeated phrase "if you really loved me you would…," followed by whatever demand or proof the person speaking deems the appropriate expression of love: "If you loved me you would have sex with me more often." "If you loved me you would be sensitive to my desire not to have sex so often." "If you loved me you would not work so many hours and not attend to me." "If you loved me you would work much harder so that my life would be materially so much easier." The list is endless, totally relative to cultural presuppositions, and, needless to say, totally beside the point, if we are talking about love and not just some social covenant between people based on the myths of obligation and the threat of condemnation and criticism should those obligations not be fulfilled.

As Medea surrenders her beliefs, one by one, so does her rage extinguish itself. Anger and rage are simply the expressions of unhappiness over not getting what we want. As mentioned earlier in the book, these emotions are attempts to motivate self and others to give us what we want, or to remind ourselves that we must pursue what we want, or that we are somehow "entitled" to what we want. In my own experience with educating people about their beliefs, I have often encountered the "Medea" complex over love turned to hate. Hate, it can be noted, is the feeling we feel when we are not getting what we want and we believe someone "should or ought to" give it to us. Our hate of that person is a measure of our outrage at their refusal to cooperate with our wants. Often, we will believe the other to be "evil" which is another way of saying "worthy of hatred" because they are not responding to our demands for what we want. Such a feeling, as we can see, can lead to limitless acts of violence when there is a feeling that all in the universe hangs upon our either forcing others to do our will or, short of that, destroying them utterly for not being what we want them to be, or for their simply being who they are!

Again the Option questions can be clarifying in knowing the truth about love and in dissipating what we may feel are inevitable feelings of hate. Knowing WHAT WE ARE UNHAPPY ABOUT, WHAT ABOUT THAT MAKES US UNHAPPY, and WHAT WE THINK IT WOULD

MEAN ABOUT US IF WE WERE NOT UNHAPPY ABOUT THAT, can be wonderfully liberating.

This was the case with a woman who came to me in great distress because her husband had announced he was leaving. There was a laundry list of complaints about her over the ten or so years of their marriage, including her frequent depressions, moodiness and demanding ways. She was in pain, in tears and filled with guilt, on the one hand, for being the inadequate woman she always suspected she was, and, on the other, filled with rage that this man would leave "after all she had done and sacrificed for him!"

In the same way as Medea, when queried as to what it would mean about her were she not to be crushed by her husband's leaving, she responded that it would indeed mean that she had never loved him! When she could see that her love had nothing to do with her unhappiness, i.e., the cultural "unconscious" imperative that unhappiness accompany loss or rejection, then she moved on to deal with the next level of beliefs about unhappiness, i.e., what is wrong with me that I am not loved by this person who is "supposed" to love me! The discussion above about the nature of love translated into Option questions became a liberating experience for her. Here is a quote that speaks to the apparently thorny, contradictory world of loving and hating, liking and not liking:

People do not feel contradictory feelings or desires. The belief that they do is frightening. People are the living resolution of apparent contradictions. For example: "I love him, but I hate him. What's wrong with me? I hate that I love him." There need not be any fear of unhappiness here. There is no paradox. You don't like what you don't like about him, and you do like some things that you do like about him. That is the way you want to feel about him. When some of those things you don't like are also the very same things you like, there is still no contradiction. What you don't like you don't like simply for the reasons you don't like it. What you do like about those same things you like only for the reasons you do like them. It is still true that you like what you like for the reasons *you like it, and don't for the reason you don't. There is nothing wrong with you, is there, if you tell the whole simplicity of the truth?*8

And so, the rhythms of Medea flow through the world of everyday existence. Like her we could come to know our happiness is beyond the reach of the behaviors and judgements of those around us, no matter how "significant" they might be defined to be in our current psychological parlance.

Chapter Five

Death, Fear and Regret.

Tolstoy's "Death of Ivan Ilych" Revisited

In this work by Tolstoy, the original purpose was to show the vacuity of a life not rooted in self examination and compassion. Tolstoy saw his world filled with what he considered the futile, superficial insincerities of empty, pretentious people. Ivan Ilych was to be a distillation of so many of these superficial traits, a man who, caught short by the advent of a mortal illness, would learn the true nature of life through his suffering. We will enter the work near the endpoint of the story. After many travails, a marriage that, like all marriages in Tolstoy's view, has become a loveless sham, Ivan has achieved a fair amount of success in the judicial system. But at this "pinnacle" of his life, he is suddenly, mysteriously struck down with what we would understand to be cancer. The disease is relentless in its course, and no medical interventions can stem its inevitable outcome. Stunned and terrified by his impending doom, stalked unceasingly by gnawing pain, Ivan lies on his deathbed, like an insect skewered on a collectors pin, writhing in the final agonies of existential dread.

Remembrance and Regret

Time took its merciless toll on Ivan as he lay in his hopeless posture staring at the ceiling, hardly daring to breathe, so as not to incur the tortures that each breath called forth in the midsection of his body. Questions tore fiercely through his mind in what seemed a ceaselessly repetitive cycle: "Why the Pain?" "Why me?" "How can a life come to this?" "There must be some mistake."

Yet, at each turn, Ivan could come up with no answers that made sense, or that made any difference. Like a tune that will not leave our awareness, pieces of old teachings and remembrances circulated through his feverish imagination. The syllogism "All men are mortal. Caius is a man. Therefore Caius is mortal," reverberated in his foggy mind as if to challenge him with the almost realized embodiment of that once abstract and formerly distant bit of classroom knowledge. Vignettes, snatches, scenes from his childhood flashed, at times with startling, vivid intensity, through his feverish brain. At those times, he was occasionally so taken up with the experience that he forgot his agonies. There he was as a babe being taken fresh from a bath, his body rosy and brimming full of health and vitality, every sensation at least a secret pleasure, with the promise of new and interesting things to come at every corner of his life. The textures, the smells, the sounds, the changing landscape of all he experienced seemed so pregnant with expanding possibilities. Nothing could be seen on the horizon to stifle the joyful, overflowing cauldron of his curiosity about all that is. All was well then, was it not? There were no demands, no pressures, no career, no wife, no children to mar the face of that most wonderful moment. Even later, as a child, the pleasant smell of his aunt's irresistible confections filled his nose with transports of delight and a warm, loving feeling accompanied that vision. Yes, it was true, the farther back in time he went, the more simple, straightforward, and direct existence seemed to be. There was a balance between him and all the world at that time. Yet, as he progressed forward in his memories, the lustre of the early potential seemed to tarnish. There were good things and bad things and a growing, seemingly endless list of do's and don'ts that brought a bewildering variety of rewards and punishments, often contradictory in nature.

He clearly recalled his experience of his own sexuality at puberty and the shame attendant upon his secret experimentations. Yet, later, he was encouraged to indulge himself discretely in sensual pursuits, so that he might be a properly rounded young man of the world. A good deal of dissembling was increasingly in order as the necessary price for maintaining decorum. He would with one breath decry certain behaviors, while at another time engage in them himself with congenial friends, who themselves would criticize the selfsame conduct in their public life. And, as he chose the law as his career, he came to see that one had to adopt a certain attitude toward reality if one was to prosper and advance.

And so he progressed, letting life shape him and mold his responses, like an actor rehearsing a part and becoming more and more adept at portraying the role that he allowed to be written for him. It was indeed that way in the matter of his marriage to Praskovya Fedorovna, a young woman of not unprepossessing looks and material advantages, but neither was she the object of any intense or particular passion, that is to say, beyond the normal range of what his female attractions had been up to this point. But there she was, having fallen into his path, so to say, at just the proper moment when marriage was considered most suitable and most appropriate for a young, rising government official such as himself. So why not?

Marriage became a hard school indeed for Ivan, requiring as it did, most especially after the arrival of the first child, his attendance to innumerable details that heretofore had not encumbered his comfortably flowing life. The fragile veneer of pleasure and politeness that had marked their courtship was rent asunder by her constant states of pique and apparently interminable list of demands on his time and affections. While at first he attempted to negotiate this difficulty almost as if it were a complex court case that called for all his adversarial and ingratiating skills, it soon became clear that marriage was not a legal brief to be resolved by a set course of logic, but that it was some other entity, some deeper and, for Ivan, hopelessly enigmatic human experience before which the formerly unfailing skills of his schooling in the affairs of human conduct had left him totally unprepared.

Abandoning reasonable discourse, he introduced *force majeure*, he raised his voice, threatened, cajoled, pleaded, asserted his husbandly magisterial authority and, ultimately, exited the scene by going to a card game with friends, or locking himself in his study under the pretext of pressing demands of state business.

He felt truly aggrieved at his wife's unseemly outbreaks and her accusations of lack of love. Often, he heard the dreaded phrase "if you loved me you would" followed by some specific thing that Ivan had either shown lack of interest in, insufficient sensitivity about, or simply had, for reasons that seemed clearly malevolent from his wife's perspective, refused to do for her. His counterattacks, much more weakly organized to be sure, and uniformly without obvious effect, came also to include that phrase; yet, he could not find within himself that apparently bottomless sense of victimization, entitlement and righteous hatred that seemed to body forth in abundance in his wife, or for that matter in all women in so far as he knew.

Fortunately, his most powerful ploy, that of evasion, ignoring and most of all of drowning himself in his official duties, eventually led to a standoff. His wife seemed finally to acknowledge that she could not get him to do what she wanted no matter how intense she made her displeasure with him known and so, without ever a word actually being spoken about the matter, they came to that most blessed of situations: they left each other entirely alone! Except for details of the household, occasional flights of erotic adventure, that only added to the number of mouths to feed and were soon swallowed up again in the vast ocean of discontents, there was no discourse that did not fit the acceptable framework of what was decorous and appropriate. Angry and embarrassing moments there were, but they were mercifully brief and equilibrium was soon restored.

Thus Ivan's life, thrown slightly off course for a number of years, soon began to gain back its familiar, comfortable rhythms, not that Ivan could say he was happy, exactly, but rather that the inevitable disappointments of existence were under control, and did not often exceed the bounds of the tolerable. So it went until the day the pain appeared, only as a minor dull ache to be sure, not even one for which he deigned to seek official medical attention when he was sure that simple home remedies would do. Yet, as the pain made it clear it would not accede to such an uncomplicated approach, he was prevailed upon to seek the counsel of a physician. This calm and composed professional, the first in a long line of such who would prod, poke, pry and peer into every possible corner of his body that would yield itself to the technology of the time, was initially totally reassuring and Ivan left believing that all would be well; it was just a matter of medicine and dietary regime for the body to slough off this mere pest of an ache. However, this pain proved to be as unreasonable in its own way as his wife had been in hers. It would not heed the judgements of the experts about its fleeting and innocent nature. It could not be disposed of in a lawful manner as was the case in the law courts over which Ivan, now a magistrate of some import, presided. It required only that he, as the governing authority, and of course in accordance with legal precedent, peer down at whatever miscreant were to be brought before him and decide that creature's fate. With the flourish of a pen and with the recitation of the related legal text, Ivan was used to dispensing with the unwanted flotsam and jetsam of human society; yes, the "pains" of the body politic would inevitably yield to his decisions and his legal surgeries assured the health of the community at large, a fact from which he drew his own personal satisfaction.

Would that it were only so in the matter of the human corpus. Here, evidently, other factors were at work that increasingly seemed to escape the ken of doctors, whose reputations grew, in direct proportion with their fees, as he sought a wider and wider circle of experts to deliver him from his pain, as he was wont to do in his law court for the social body. Their uniform failure to offer any relief gradually came to confirm Ivan's worst suspicions; that for some reason *he* had become the accused, for the pain was nested in him and his fate seemed totally tied to the fate of whatever flaw in him that pain represented. It was as if, he, most assuredly completely upright and innocent of any offence, were somehow shackled to this errant inner organ that refused to follow the innate natural laws of the body and further adamantly refused to be corrected by the lawful authorities of the physicians, for which it was to be condemned to the ultimate punishment. Ivan, for his part could understand this condemnation, nay he felt a solidarity with their frustration and impatience. But, there was the small matter of his unbreakable tie to this criminal tissue, which meant that this condemned's turn at the gallows would be simultaneously his as well.

He longed to cry out how unfair it all was. He was innocent, innocent, and yet his fate was sealed and beyond his control. Now he lay in that cell of the condemned, whose confines were his own physical self, and waited for the course of the law to carry it on to final execution. How disgusting and crude it all came to be at the last. All the refinements of life, the pleasures, the clever conversations, the minor seductions, the triumphs of office politics, the praise of superiors, all of it came to naught and vanished before the barbaric might of fleshy vulnerability. Further, as he sat in his corporeal prison, all around him, sensing his relationship to the offending organ and the import of same, began to take their distance from him. So called friends and intimates presented themselves with diminishing frequency and sat, discomforted in obligatory good cheer to which he felt obliged himself to respond as if his fate were not his fate. He felt what he perceived to be the further affront of the meaninglessness of all that he had prized as important and conducive to a polite and civilized existence, and yet he still felt constrained by the logic of this now useless regimen of existence to ape its rules and to maintain the prescribed external demeanor. The raw business of physical dissolution, like a hardened convict accustomed to the insults, injuries and rapacious manners of incarceration, bore relentlessly down upon him, seeming to enjoy his terror and helplessness, taunting him with further hints of still unspeakable horrors to come. Ivan's heart shriveled up in the manner of the righteously wronged. He turned from all around him and gave himself over to his despair without reserve. The only person whom he let near him to tend to his increasingly embarrassing and gross physical needs was a manservant, Gerasim, a person of middle age, strong of build, sure of foot and completely at ease with what were for Ivan, unbearable ministrations. Often, Gerasim would just sit with Ivan and massage his legs or be a silent comfortable presence. Ivan queried him about his role:

"Is this not difficult for you Gerasim, dealing with this mess, its odor and everything about such a sickness?"

"Not at all sir. It's all a part of being human."

"But, my God, was humanity meant to be this appalling travesty?"

"What about this situation most disturbs you sir?"

"The essential unfairness of it all, how I was so brutally plucked out of my life and thrust into the anteroom of oblivion."

"With all respect sir, death will come to us all. So in what way do you experience your dying as unfair?"

Ivan was taken aback with the question and a gleam of anger flashed in his eyes, but the manner of the question was so gentle and patient that this feeling instantly dissolved and he gazed at the kindly face of the servant for a moment before responding:

"I'm sure it is all relative Gerasim; in any event, I should not be burdening you with my complaints, you have borne much on my behalf already as it is."

"It's no trouble sir. Sometimes to see the plain truth can relieve one, so if you wish to talk I'll be most happy to listen or to respond if you would like."

However, just then, Gerasim was called away by Ivan's wife for some other purpose, and subsequently had to leave for the country estate to ready it should Ivan last until the spring, so that the initial conversation begun that day did not continue. Yet, somehow, Gerasim's questions pro-voked Ivan's interest. Naturally, Gerasim was just a simple servant, unschooled and incapable of any real intellectual discourse, yet, there was a native intuition about his whole demeanor and his words that indis-putably attracted Ivan.

Bereft now of even this simple soul to console him, Ivan found himself bound deeper into the dark chambers of his anguish. Indeed, it was very much like a sack into which he felt thrust, with nothing but the pain and the blackness as his companions. He cried out in his terror. "Why? What do you want of me?" Silence ensued and then, all of a sudden, a voice, clear and resonant, replied:

"Nothing, All is as it is."

"No!" shouted back Ivan soundlessly from deep within the sack, "No, all is not as it is, not as it should be, it cannot be this way."

Silence. "Nothing, nothing, it was nothing after all," thought Ivan, when again the voice sounded:

"What about the way things are makes you unhappy?"

Ivan froze, debating whether to engage in a response, fearful lest the voice disappear and leave him alone. He shouted in his silence: "To be ripped untimely from the bosom of my life. This is an outrage. Have I not lived my life as I was directed to, as I ought to, have I not observed all the laws and mores? Why then was I so wrongfully used?"

"What do you mean when you say you lived your life as you 'ought to'?"

"Just look at my life. Was I not little Ivan, that relished the berries on my uncle's estate in early August, that ran with the dogs across the mead-ows? Were not all my relations at home and in the law court as they should have been? In what way then do I deserve this fate?"

"What do you mean when you say 'deserve'?"

"How else could this all have come about? Do not the wicked and the guilty deserve such agonies? How do I come to such a pass?"

"What do you mean by the 'wicked' and the 'guilty'?"

"Why, I know the law," retorted Ivan vehemently, "I know wrongdoers and people of evil inclination. I have been privy to the most minute details of their horrendous deeds. Such agonies as I have experienced surely belong to them, for having done what they have done."

"In what way were what you call the 'wicked' and the 'guilty' doing anything other than what they knew to do based on what they believed?"

"You think to challenge me on the law? The texts are clear, that what they were believing is irrelevant. The deed alone determines their culpability and the consequences that follow."

"The consequences may be whatever an age determines them to be for human actions, the question remains, in what way were they doing other than what they believed at the instant of their actions?"

"They could have, no should have, known otherwise and followed more noble instincts than the ones they chose to follow."

"In what way could they have done otherwise if at the moment they acted they were acting on what in that instant represented what they believed? Can you both choose and not choose to do something at one and the same instant?"

"No it is true," reflected back Ivan, "you choose your actions moment to moment, one action at a time. But, even granting this to be the case, their actions, be they the best they knew at the moment they knew it, might be and, in the cases I make reference to, were evil and unspeakable."

"What do you mean by evil?"

"That they were terrible, the kind of activities that turn the stomach or cause the hearts of civilized people to break for pity of the victims and their loved ones."

"Are you saying that you were personally upset or angry about these acts?"

"Why yes of course. I abhor the acts and the vile creatures who perpetrated them. It was my pleasure to consign them to the heaviest strictures our laws permit."

"What specifically about the deeds and the those who did them draws forth your ire so deeply?" Ivan puzzled over the question and said: "I don't know what else to say beyond what I have explained."

"Do you think it would mean anything about you were you not to be enraged and distressed by these people and their acts?"

"Surely I would not only be delinquent as an officer of the court in not pursuing my duties appropriately, but, more personally, I would be some kind of unthinking, unfeeling wretch to be indifferent to such men as these and their deeds. It would be tantamount to condoning such actions were I to be without feeling in the matter."

"Are you saying that your way to ensure that you maintain appropriate concern for deeds such as this is to feel the pain of your anger and distress so as not to forget?"

Ivan pondered the question for a moment and said:

"I have never considered my feelings in this way before, but, yes, as I think about it, there is a sense in which it seems that the concern and the pain connected to it seem a seamless unity, that there cannot be one without the other."

"Are you saying that you do not know that you are against such acts as you refer to without the agonies of anger and distress to buttress your knowledge?"

"It is more, as I pass it through my experience, that it would be unseemly to simply know it without the accompanying feelings."

"What do you mean?"

"That the feelings express your dedication to the common, civilized consensus about such actions and, were they lacking, that people would find you wanting in authenticity in the expression of your opposition to such deeds."

"Are you saying that without the painful feelings, you would not be perceived as a 'good' or 'caring' person?"

"That seems to me to be so when you put it like that."

"And what about not being perceived so might upset you?"

Ivan felt the intensity of that question at the root of his experience of himself and resisted the inferences that arose in him as a response: "I have lived my life in conformity with what the best in society have considered decorous and in taste. Except for the most minor deviations, my life has been an exemplar of propriety. I should never like to lose that image and that opinion of me on the part of others."

"And, if despite that desire, others should hold negative opinions of you?"

Ivan felt a great weight upon him holding him back, and the pain, which heretofore had been strangely absent while the voice was speaking with him, suddenly broke through with merciless ferocity: "Oh my God," he moaned" others have already abandoned me, have already consigned me to the rubbish pile. I overheard my wife in another room making funeral arrangements, imagine that, and my body not yet cold in death. I am alive, "he shouted in the darkness, "how dare you dismiss me, how dare you treat me as some inconvenient mound of rotting flesh. I will not have it, do you hear, I will not have it!"

The voice continued: "What about others acting in a way which makes their awareness of your impending death obvious distresses you?"

Ivan felt himself sobbing, racked with the deepest pain, deeper by far than the physical agony which he had railed against so long: "None of them give a damn about me? I am a mere convenience, a provider of goods and services for the nurturance of their healthy bodies and the pleasures of that body. My wife grows fat in her abundance, my daughter displays her flesh for purposes of attracting some unwary fool such as I was at her age, and my son mopes around looking constantly disappointed and ashamed of something. If they loved me surely they would declare this to me in a convincing way, surely they would weep for my pain, surely they would find a way to help alleviate my grief. But no. They move and have their being and to hell with me. They are discomforted that I have had the bad taste to stay around so long. I display my bad taste by holding on to what shred of life I may still find possible to maintain."

"Why do you believe that their following the course of their own beliefs about what is best for them to do under the circumstances means that they do not love you at least insofar as those beliefs allow them to manifest that love?"

"Ach, you mean that like the criminals we spoke of earlier, they are doing the best they know how given what they believe?"

"Was that not so for you when you were healthy and were relating to those around you according to what you considered the best dictates of taste and decorum?"

Ivan recoiled at the voice's question, but responded:

"Oh but that is the worst, you see, don't you, that I lost my life by never being any more than a puppet to what was currently acceptable, by never taking any risks lest I offend or put off those whose influence and good offices I sought to gain. I never loved but so cautiously and defensively because I never wanted anyone to gain the upper hand on me, or to take advantage of me. I treated my life as a court case to be lived in a clever and adversarial manner, so that I would have the control. And now it is too late. I have been all too successful, for those I would have close to me are now but reflections of my own point of view. They view *me* the way that I have viewed *them*! They have learned from me, and from their own experiences too, I suppose, all too well. What I most yearn for now, I have made impossible."

"Are you saying that you were not acting from your own beliefs at the time you did what you did, given everything you understood in all the instants you actually did what you did?"

"No, no, noooooo," shouted Ivan to the voice: "I will not let myself off the hook so cheaply. I have made a mockery of what a life should be and now my fate is sealed. Now I understand my suffering, it is deserved, I *am* the criminal worthy of condemnation and execution. No mercy is called for, and yet I yearn for mercy."

"What are you afraid would happen were you to let go of your condemnation of yourself?"

"What, and let the criminal go free? I will not play the hypocrite and apply a different standard of justice to myself than what I applied to those that stood before my bench. My life is my responsibility and now I see how empty and superficial it was."

"Are you saying that if you were to let go of your self-hatred you would not know that you do not like what your life has become?"

Ivan continued to be racked by sobs and pain, the emotional and the physical alternating in a synergy of boundless discomfort. Yet, here was a clarity beginning to dawn in his mind. "Why must I see my painful feelings as inevitable? But how to change if not through them? Wait, am I saying that my miseries are the key to transformation? Such unhappiness as I have had, the ones that I have openly acknowledged, and the ones that I denied, they never brought anything but dissemblance, distance, and enforced superficiality, the very things that now I seem to writhe in agony over. Will my further agonies effect what a life of chronic and hidden pains failed to accomplish?"

And he responded to the voice: "Bear with me oh voice, my companion, are you saying that all suffering is of our own making, for our own purposes, whether to upbraid ourselves or others for unwanted actions or to coerce ourselves or others to do what we want done?"

"How do you feel about that?"

"As I see it now it would imply that no state of feeling is in itself necessary or inevitable, but that we decide it to be so; that nothing is either good nor bad, nor evil in itself, but that we declare it to be so. And, that we do this for our own good reasons, based on what we have believed and now believe, what the world around us defines to be so, or to have the quality of creating the emotional consequences of unhappiness within us, given that we are in agreement with that and are therefore allowing those consequences to have that effect within us. Yes, my life from its earliest moments had that quality. The farther back I went in my memories, the less encumbered I was by such experiences, but in direct proportion to my maturity, I found myself somehow mysteriously woven into a web of responses that seemed organic, natural to each given moment and context, and yet tinged with a sense of frustration and, yes, even despair, that somehow things could never be otherwise because the causes were beyond our control, in others, in events themselves."

"And how do you feel about that?"

Ivan still felt the great weight holding him back from moving deeper into the sack, a direction that he had dreaded, but now felt somehow attracted to. The pains raged on: "Yes, yes, it is clearer now, but still, to admit my life to have been lived in the grips of such beliefs and now even given some enlightenment, I am thrust to its very end and have but the briefest moment to know something different."

"What about that distresses you?"

"There is so much I would wish to savor, so much I would wish to do differently were there only the time."

"And if there is no time?"

"Then there is…" and Ivan's inner voice halted, choked on the word, "there is death."

"And what about death do you fear?"

"I will not be, there will be no me to live the life I would want to live?"

"What about not having the opportunity to do that distresses you?"

"Dearest voice, simply that I would have it so."

"And if you were not distressed about whatever you might not have, nor ever had in your life?"

Suddenly there was silence, not in the sense of sound, but wait, there was no pain, no pain of feelings, no pain of body; all seemed in a moment of suspension. Ivan wondered at this and then attended to the voice's question: "Then, then…, then I would approve of what I am, how I am, even now at this moment?"

"Are you saying you would rather not know what you now have come to know?"

"No, dearest voice, no. I am filled with gratitude now for that knowledge."

"Then why would you hold back your full approval of who and what you are?"

"Somehow, I continue to think of all the moments past and how they were not what they might have been had I known what I know now."

"Why do you believe your life was anything but exactly what it should have been, given your beliefs and how you manifested them from moment to moment?"

"So, yes, that is true, but what of those around me, I still long to ask their forgiveness for how I have offended them and deprived them of what might have been?"

"If, as you have affirmed, it is true for you that your life was perfect, that is, it was exactly as it should have been given what you believed, then why would you believe it would be any different for those around you?"

Ivan paused, the silence of feelings and bodily pangs remained, and he responded with a brilliant flash of awe and wonderment: "Perhaps that is what true compassion is then."

"What do you mean?"

"That there is nothing to judge, for all are doing the best they know to do."

"And what of forgiveness?"

Ivan began to feel the great stone weight that held him fast in the sack slowly diminish in its hold as he articulated the words:

"True forgiveness then, is knowing that there is nothing to forgive. So then my life has been and continues to be the best life I know to have, even though I would still have it that there would be many more moments to live it out."

"But Ivan," intoned the voice in a manner that resonated symphonically as if a thousand voices were echoing the same refrain all around him: "how do you feel *now, in this very moment!*"

"Ahhhhhhhh," responded Ivan in what seemed an endless sigh of realization, "there is no other now but now and I have full possession of it, Ahhhhhhhhh," and with that the stone weight fell away and Ivan was released into the bottom of the sack and fell, soft like a feather on the breath of God.

*****"And death....where is it?"

He sought his former accustomed fear of death, and did not find it. "Where is it? What death?" There was no fear...there was no death.

In place of death there was light.

"So that's what it is!" he suddenly exclaimed aloud. "What joy!"

To him all this happened in a single instant, and the meaning of that instant did not change. For those present his agony continued for another two hours. Something rattled in his throat, his emaciated body twitched, then the gasping and rattle became less and less frequent.

"It is finished!" said someone near him.

He heard these words and repeated them in his soul. "Death is finished," he said to himself. "it is no more!" He drew in a breath, stopped in the midst of a sigh, stretched out, and died.

***** From this point to the end taken verbatim from a translation of the short story by Tolstoy, from The Death of Ivan Ilych and Other Stories, Signet paperback, 1960.

Final Things

The questions raised by this chapter resonate at the deepest levels for most people. The character of our lives is drawn on the fabric of cultural, social and familial expectations that we have made our own. As our lives evolve, and particularly as we fail to achieve whatever idiosyncratic landmark accomplishments we believe to be the proofs of a life worthily lived, we can create a slough of despond, a swamp of regrets, a sense of the *unbearable wrongness of being*.

Additionally, as we approach the end point of our lives, whether simply by dint of age or, as in this work, due to some disease that we cannot turn around, the potential pain of both dimensions can amplify our despair, given of course the beliefs we hold at any particular time.

We also see, as in the story, how accumulated beliefs about life can create a deepening "sink hole" of certainties about the meaninglessness of life. The confusion Ivan suffers derives from conflicting belief imperatives that quickly overshadow the remembered simplicity and freedom of his earliest years. The duplicities required to advance himself in the world, the utter clash of assumptions and their apparent inability to be resolved that resided in the conventional arrangement called a marriage, the felt "need" to withdraw and to avoid, all these processes of belief created a web of entanglements that he felt completely choked and trapped by when faced with the unyielding truth of mortal illness.

Note, that in the original, pain was to be a "teacher" to force Ivan to see the "error" of his ways and the meaninglessness of his life. In our version, pain is no teacher, merely the gauge of how vigorously he holds on to the beliefs that torture him so relentlessly. Surrendering the beliefs is to let go of the pain, or to see pain for what it is, a physiological phenomena, not a punishment or experience requiring unhappiness.

Having worked in the past with people in Ivan's place, i.e., facing the likelihood of death from illness, I have seen that people not only live but also die by their beliefs. Before I came to know Option as a personal reality for myself, I would view such experiences as "tragic." What I have noticed is that to the degree my attitude changed about life and death, the quality of my work with people in this situation also changed. People could know, like Ivan, that each moment is absolute in itself and that it takes only an instant to know one's happiness. For those who did choose to know this, their passing was qualitatively different from those who remained steeped in their sense of dread, regret and horror over their impending death.

"The Horror, The Horror": Fears, Phobias, the Dread of Dread

In Conrad's The *Heart of Darkness*, when the narrator finally finds the object of his search in the depths of 19th century Africa, that person, Kurz, sums up his experience of life (his abandonment of the myths of European civility and the adoption of the power myths of tribal mores with all the subsequent destruction of life to feed that power) with the words "The horror! The horror!"

The prime issue, as reviewed earlier in different contexts, is the fear of evil, that is of being against oneself:

The belief in evil is the belief that people can be against themselves, and that, moreover, even by their will or against their will. Either possibility is, by turn, depressing or frightening. The belief in evil is no more than the fear that people can be against their own values, and therefore unhappy against their will. The belief that unhappiness in any or all of its forms can 'happen' or be caused to an unwilling person, is the cause of all unhappiness in the person who believes thus.9

Fear is always metachronic, that is prospective. It is anticipation of unhappiness at some future time when it is assumed we will have to be unhappy about some hypothesized event or experience that will "cause" such experiences to come to be in us. Thus it is that the standard vision of causality is reversed from an Option perspective. We are not "caused" to do things by virtue of what has happened to us in our past. The past is always the information we now at this moment possess about ourselves as mediated by what we believe. We look out to the future through the "eyes" of our beliefs, and as we perceive events moving toward us, we make decisions based upon what we believe those events to mean. If we believe that we have to be unhappy about such experiences, then, of course, that is what we are; if we are open to the moment and have let go of our beliefs in the necessity of unhappiness, then the moment becomes whatever we make of it out of that happiness.

Those That Do Not Learn from the Future Are Doomed to Repeat It!

Having thus defined the nature of fear, we can better understand the origins of what are called dread experiences, phobias, fears of every stamp. If we were to know that we are perfectly free to make the decision and to have the "desire to be cautious or avoid something," then phobias could never arise in the first place. However, we are taught, or come to believe that we "should" have some different outlook on whatever it is we wish to be cautious about. People might wish to avoid or be cautious in certain social situations, or when they are at great heights, or in the water, on bridges, tunnels etc. etc., the list is endless.

Being told, or coming to believe, as noted, that such caution or avoidance is abnormal or not appropriate behavior can lead us to believe that this is another case of where we are "bad" for ourselves:

When they believe they are wrong to feel that way, and believe that they should not have such strong feelings of caution, that conflict is what is called the fear. It feels like one SHOULD recklessly endanger oneself even though one has no such desire. A person comfortable with their own sense of caution; who does not feel challenged to 'overcome' their so-called fear, will not feel the fear....10

One woman described to me the origins of her fear. She was required to go to a social function with people whom she knew were engaged in a variety of betrayals of her trust. Rather than trusting her own sense of caution and standing her ground about not going (she was an adult at the time), she acquiesced because she believed that she "should" overcome her own sense of caution and do what others thought was best. The result was a "mysterious" appearance of "panic" attacks.

Still another woman came who had begun to have the classic signs of agoraphobia in a sudden onset. Again, she was in a situation that she felt demanded her to act against her own self interests, her own sense of caution, and she could not find it within herself to identify the acculturated beliefs that put her in such conflict with herself. When she did, she dispensed with the incipient fears within a few days! The crucial sense of inner congruity is what is lacking in the illusion that we could ever somehow be against ourselves:

The truth that unhappy people believe they should not accept about them-
selves is the very truth that is intrinsic to a living, wanting being; an otherwise
wise and intelligent creature. I am FOR what I am for, and I am AGAINST
what I am against, and it can not be different. In other words, I like (want)
what I like, and don't like(want) what I don't like. I can't be wrong. That is
just the way it is. Even if I were now to be for what I used to be against, I
would still be now for what I am now for, or the converse. To quote Martin
Luther, "God help me. Here I stand. I can do no other." We are exactly as we
wish to be, and would choose to be. We are exactly what we are glad to be. And
we can't do anything about that. We wouldn't want to. We don't need to. That
is meaningless. We simply won't, can't or want to be other than gladly our-
selves.... Just because we change our minds it doesn't mean we could or should
have changed our minds before we did. That only seems to make sense to those
who are already believing that we could have done that: i.e., been against
something while we were for it, or the contrary.11

Thus, whether we are talking about the Dread of Death or some other
circumstance that seems to call forth intense fear, we could know that by
gently pursuing our beliefs, by utilizing the Option questions, we could
drop our beliefs into the sea and soar into horizons of our own making on
the wings of our equanimity.

Chapter Six

"Eudaemonia": a "Lost" Dialogue of Plato on the Origins of Happiness

It is perhaps fitting in these last two chapters that we explore the notion of happiness in the setting of two ancient thinkers. In this chapter, we turn to Socrates and to the famous dialogues recorded by Plato. The choice is somewhat obvious, because the Option method is a dialogue, a series of questions designed to aid people in discovering what is already theirs, but which they have not yet admitted into their knowing. This in some way reflects the vision of Socrates who thought that we all had knowledge of the universe present in ourselves and that his task was merely to aid in your own discovery of what you possessed. His method was a questioning process. In this fictional version, I, of course, have Socrates change his philosophical position and "discover" the Option truths about the nature of happiness.

Present are friends of Socrates, Antisthenes, founder of the School of Cynicism, Alcibiades, statesman and old drinking friend, Aristophanes, the playwright and comic poet, and Eryximachos, a physician.

Socrates: How good it is to be with you once again, to salute the spring with the early fruits of the earth and seasoned wine.

Alcibiades: Ah, dear friend, the wine particularly has drawn me to you. For despite your renown in matters arcane, much of which escapes me anyhow, you remain a master in your choice of the subtleties of the grape.

Aristophanes: for all his subtlety in selecting it, there is but small subtlety in your quaffing it.

Alcibiades: Save your witticisms for the theater, for none here need be impressed by your talents. Besides, is not wine good physic for the body, learned physician?

Eryximachos: There are many things that promote the body's health, but they are best taken in some balanced way. Wine in proportion can increase the forces of vitality, but in surfeit it can defeat the selfsame inclination.

Antisthenes: Well said, and fully in the spirit of using balance to say nothing. Such words are often the most useful medicines in the healer's pharmacy, for they do artfully disguise the woeful lack in the physician's art.

Socrates: Friends, friends, you seem bent on conjuring up discord, while I have brought you here to discourse on happiness, a theme that has drawn me in some special way of late, as passions in the polis build against me for my alleged corrupted ways.

Alc.: Former friends often become the most envenomed foes; but rest at ease, your vindication cannot be in doubt. Do not trouble yourself over petty rancor and jealousies.

Soc.: Many thanks for your good wishes, but your remarks in truth do reflect my meditations directly, for I find nothing in the ill will of others nor in events themselves to quell my felicity.

Aris.: The consequences of the ire of those who seek to harm you may indeed be grave. Surely some tremor of anticipation must break the tranquility of your hours even though you maintain your good feelings as you may.

Soc.: What do you think is worthy of upset in this, dear poet?

Aris.: I would not speak for you in this matter, but for myself, the prospect of severe, even mortal civil punishment is sufficient food for thought to bend my spirits to dark musings and disquieting emotions.

Soc.: Ah, excellent. So then within your statement is contained the kernel of my discovery. First, you speak prospectively, that is your mind considers what "could" or "might" be, things that are as yet but shadows in your imagination, and yet, these shadows do cast themselves in your experience as present pains and do thereby diminish or extinguish the light of your present joys. Next in order for your mind to consider anything at all, it does so by virtue of how it has organized itself to consider things, that is, through a system of beliefs. It is your beliefs, then, that shape and give feeling substance to what you perceive, is that not so?

Antis.: That is so, or would seem to be the most likely course for human actions, but if it be as you describe, then what of those who seek the Good, the Virtuous, the Beautiful? What rule shall guide them in the formation of those beliefs, so that they have true discernment of what is proper?

Soc.: Much have I given thought to my former views about the pursuit of what I have called the Good in the creation of virtue; things now seem otherwise than I had earlier divined. Let me attempt to illustrate. What do you mean by the "Good," Antisthenes?

Antis.: Why, that which reflects the "idea" of the Good most perfectly.

Soc.: And what do you mean by the "idea" of the Good?

Antis.: Why that which you yourself on many occasions have described as the utmost quality of a thing excluding all the limitations of any particular version of it.

Soc.: That being the case, then, the good would be recognized by the individual knowers manifesting what they perceived at any time to be the good, is that not so?

Antis.: That is indeed true as to the real experience of humans in their moment to moment actions, but it leaves unresolved the question of what the good is in itself, for good is determined to be so by many peoples each in their own way and for their own purposes.

Soc.: Precisely so, dear thinker, for each in their own way acts according to their version of the good as it presents itself to them out of the mind's assessment of the situation according to their beliefs.

Antis.: But that leaves a cacophony of different goods arising from so many different minds, each one insisting on how they see being to be at any given moment. Surely harmony and felicity cannot exist in such a condition as this. Was that not why you sought to define the good and the virtuous originally, to provide humans with a path out of such a painful disorder as this?

Soc.: You are correct dear student, but the wise man is he who accepts true wisdom from any source. And what better source than one's own inspiration to find a better way. Earlier I sought to move humans to the good by having them attracted by what I then perceived to be a pure and unadulterated notion of the good. But my observations of others, but most particularly of myself, have moved me to understand things other-wise. For, human societies have been of uniform mind and like purpose and have not achieved the good. Indeed, the very concept of the good I see now to have been mistaken, for by the good I really meant happiness or felicity as the goal of human existence. In truth, I see no happiness or joy deriving from so many different communities' notions of civil virtue. To place an icon of what should be in the public eye is not to create felicity, but only to emphasize the distance of average citizens from how they ought to be. Surely this is a formula for unhappiness, if felicity awaits one only in some unattainable abstraction however defined as the good, or truth or beauty.

Antis.: But is that not what the sophists teach, that nothing can truly ever be known? Is not felicity, happiness in whatever form, to be sought after and earned through the practice of virtue? Therefore, is it not our role as teachers to instruct the populace in the paths of virtue so that they might live in hope of felicity?

Soc.: Is this not the case with every land? Travelers come to us from all the regions of the earth and tell us of their notions of virtue. Have we not so many differing opinions of what the truth consists of? If virtue, which every culture and state wishes to inculcate into its citizenry, were effective in attaining what we have been calling the good, then why are peoples constantly at war with one another, and why the claims that their notions of the good are superior to all others?

Antis.: Well, then, if we are to abandon the whole notion of the "Good" then in what way will we ever attain happiness, being bereft of a guide to such attainment?

Soc.: Ah, good cynic, your question brings us back to the original concerns of our poet Aristophanes. Recall you said that your imaginings over my possible fate at the hands of the state wrought painful emotions within you.

Arist.: That is so. The mere thinking of such a fate evoked feelings that seemed to come unbidden into my body as I considered these possibilities.

Soc.: And, if you were now to think of the ideas of the "good" and the "beautiful"—however they might arise in your mind—do they allay any of those presentiments over such a fate as you imagine?

Arist.: No, in truth, I feel no difference, though I pass through my mind all your teachings on the subject, nay and the teachings of others that I have chanced upon in these many years. Thinking them as I might, my fear remains a constant at the prospect of such punishments.

Soc.: So, thinking these thoughts, whatever else their value might be, seem powerless in the face of your fears. Otherwise, your feelings would have been altered by such thoughts, is that not so?

Arist.: That would seem to be so, for there is no change.

Soc.: Then, as I earlier noted, it must be in what you believe that the cause of your fear is to be found.

Arist.: But is it not so that if you remove the external thing the fear also removes itself? The condemned live in dread but rejoice should they be pardoned and set free. The threat then does evoke the response, else why would its removal be the cause of the return of felicity?

Soc.: But, dear poet, it is not always so that a change of state or fortune also removes the fear it is purported to evoke? How many instances do we know where people live in dread though there be no source apparent to another's eyes? Have we not then to look within for what is invisible, what lives in their imaginations, even as your presentiments about my possible punishments have no actual external source or cause in this moment, but, are, as I said earlier, but shadows of what could be woven into the very fabric of fear by what you believe?

Eryx.: But what about the imagined event itself? Is not the prospect of punishment and death sufficient to draw forth agonies of anticipation in any human?

Soc.: My good doctor, are you saying that the sensations of fear, distress, sadness, grief etc., are properties of actions or things in themselves? If so, how are we to explain the great variety of human responses to so many things that many of us here this evening might define as terrible or unbearable? Would there not be a recognizable uniformity of response, given your proposed hypothesis that the emotion is somehow innate to the action or whatever thing be supposed capable of drawing forth human misery against our will? It would be against our will, would it not?

Eryx.: How do you mean?

Soc.: I mean that people do not want to be unhappy do they, even in this most extreme circumstance, or, perhaps, especially in the most extreme circumstances.

Eryx.: Well I suppose that is true, though many seem to seek unhappiness if only in the pursuit of virtue for example, where heroes will face death, or mothers will defend their young against attack.

Soc.: But would not these instances, more closely examined, disclose that their seeking of what they may consider as unhappiness is actually their way of seeking happiness? They know no other way to seek happiness or know no other choice but to believe, that they have to be unhappy as the price for some other felicity they would wish?

Alcib.: But my good friend, is it not true that our basic distress follows from our perception of the fundamental flaws and deficits of the world around us? Are these flaws not what we seek to redress when we build larger cities, monuments, change our laws, do not our poets, such as our present friend, add to the fund of what is good, true and beautiful and in essence thereby correct what is unseemly, are not our doctors adding to their knowledge of the human body to correct our lack of knowing, and is this all not by way of causing what is better to come to be and thereby to increase our felicity?

Soc.: In the cases you cite, as to the physical environment and what you describe as our improvements thereof, are these not practical goods that do not so much *perfect* what is defective as *rearrange* what is for our human convenience? Were I to happen upon a crumbling temple, perhaps a deity whose adepts had abandoned belief in her, does the physical state of that building represent a lack or a defect? No, the stone and mortar are what we have assembled for our own purposes, for nature troubles itself not at all to create dwellings. How can their existence or lack then be in any way a reflection upon nature?

Is not the same true for what we contrive to do in the state or in art or any craft that increases human convenience? How are these manifestations of our creative intelligence in any way prior to or causative of our happiness, which, like nature herself, is an innate characteristic thereof and not subject to revision by human imagination? As we discover our own nature and nature's nature, we may discern the marvelous workings of being in her endless manifestations and deepen our capacity to appreciate our happiness as a part of that, but how is our felicity ever at issue in these discoveries and their practical applications for our convenience?

Alcib.: But do we not suffer disappointments when our mores and institutions fail us, when our knowledge of the curative arts does not maintain our health, when our friends and intimates die or desert us; for are you not yourself in the shadow of such imperfections as the state is wont to effect, should the rumors prove true, and you stand accused by former friends?

Soc.: Ah, good companion, you bring us back to the realm of the personal, which alone is where felicity dwells and has its roots in our minds our beliefs and hence our feelings, for feelings are but functions of the same reality, one part manifesting in the mind as belief, the other in the body as emotions.

As to myself, I am content no matter what the state may decide. But let me query you or any among you as to what discontents you may presently hold so that you may unfold to yourself the truth that happiness is innate. Shall it be you my venerable friend who starts this inquiry?

Alcib.: Were you to ask me what at this present moment stirs up my sadness, then I would say directly that the thought of your departure from among us brings me to tears and a pall falls upon my soul.

Soc.: What about my death so saddens you?

Alcib.: For the world, that so great a mind is lost to us forever and the light of knowledge will not be lit in uncounted minds yet to be born. As it relates to me personally, that so great and true a friend will no longer be present to warm my heart and bring comfort to my fading days.

Soc.: What about my absence so distresses you?

Alcib.: Why, as I said, you shall no longer be present to give counsel, to lift my spirits.

Soc.: What about that distresses you?

Alcib.: You know me well, Socrates; I fear I shall falter in my steps as I negotiate my life and will thereby do myself in from my own bad habits.

Soc.: Are you saying that you will somehow be "bad" for yourself, and particularly will be so without me around to guide you?

Alcib.: That is the truth, sweet philosopher. I am but a barely tolerated politician now and fear what I shall become should you pass from among us. How many times have I betrayed myself, made a laughing stock of myself before the general populace. I am the worst of my enemies.

Soc.: Were you not even in all that you call self betraying behavior, were you not doing whatever you knew to do, whatever you believed, hence chose, based on the very specific moment when you acted?

Alcib.: Ah but dear lover of life, what I did was not in my best interests to do. It was not becoming a statesman to be found besotted, for in doing so I surely have lost the confidence of the people.

Soc.: Consequences may well be there for our deeds, for these are often set by nature. Should we stray too near a precipice and fall, we can be said to experience the consequences of our misstep, and, in like manner, human communities will assign different consequences to our deeds all according to their customs and beliefs. So be it. But we speak here not of consequences, but of attitudes, for they alone and not the consequences, determine our state of mind and feelings. Therefore, even if the consequences you describe were to befall you, why are you unhappy about that?

Alcib.: But does that not only prove my basic untrustworthiness, for I am the butt of the jokes of poets such as Aristophanes, even as you have been yourself, dear friend?

Soc.: And if you were not to be troubled by your behavior in this way, what are you afraid it would mean about you?

Alcib.: To be untroubled would leave me without any manner of correcting my behavior. For do we not trouble our children and instill in them both fear and shame that they might not stray from the paths of right reason and virtue and thereby dishonor themselves and their native land? This is an old wisdom, sweet philosopher, that has spoken over countless generations the good counsel of discomfort and displeasure in shaping the individuals who constitute the community at large, so that loyalty, civic zeal and lawful behavior would grace each nation and improve its fortunes. Though I have lost the favor of the public eye, my path is to merit more my own displeasure, lest my fall be yet even more precipitous.

Soc.: So, 'tis clear to you that your pain is self-created and in the service of deflecting you from false and dangerous paths?

Alcib.: Agreed.

Soc.: Yet all these years of constant self reproach, regret and pain, have they given you such good service that you see your resolution in the even more stringent application of this moral regimen?

Alcib.: What other direction dare I take, for my most grievous lack of sobriety and good sense does want of harsher measures to rein itself in, else surely I am doomed. And I should take to that hard school immediately. For without your presence, as I have asserted, my fate will assuredly be sealed.

Soc.: Would a runner who had lost a race be best served by the amputation of his foot to school his offending body in the merits of trying harder next time? And if he fail upon the next attempt (a prospect not unlikely it would seem), would then the removal of the other leg be the most likely path to eventual victory?

Alcib.: Ha ha, 'tis likely he were to run out of body parts, ere he found the winner's wreath gracing his brow. But, then, it is true, my hard schooling has not achieved any wreaths for me, though my sentiments against myself have been in private most stern and hateful.

Soc.: And if your unhappiness, no matter how harshly applied, has not kept you from unwanted consequences, how is it you believe its further application will liberate you from the same?

Alcib.: I now do most seriously doubt it would.

Soc.: What, therefore, would it mean about you were you not to be unhappy about your life and its consequences?

Alcib.: I sit before you now in a great calm, but yet like a vessel saved from storms, I seek to know how to use the calm if I am bereft of a rudder to find direction.

Soc.: In what way do you lack a "rudder" to find directions?

Alcib.: My feelings, unhappy though they may have been, were both sail and rudder to my destinies, or so it has seemed. How am I to know in what port to seek my best advantage without them?

Soc.: Are you saying that you only know your wants, your likes and dislikes through your unhappiness? When your first child was born, was it through your pain that you did know your love for that babe? When you first beheld the golden isles of the Aegean, was it from your agony that you knew of the great pleasure you experienced and your wonderful desire to return as often as you might to taste that landscape again?

Alcib.: No, no, my feelings were joyful and certain. There was no trace of sadness to dim those sweet occasions, and many others that now do flood in upon my memory. So, then, I could, and do know what directions I might take without the sting of misery's whip to prompt my purposes.

Soc.: And how do you feel about that?

Alcib.: In truth, I would have said the wine had stirred my spirits, except we have not taken a sufficient amount to support such sentiments; yet is there a giddiness that must arise from the knowing that my life's felicity is never more secure than by what I now know.

Arist.: But hold, Socrates, how can it be that the surrender of all our private hurts and distress can lead us to felicity? Were I to attain satisfaction, how would I be moved to any activity, either in the service of myself or of the state? Would not my ongoing happiness deprive me of the grating awareness necessary to make difficult discriminations on my own behalf?

Soc.: Well, dear poet, let us see. Were you not the one that said that you were in present pain over the imagined punishments that I might suffer at some future time?

Arist.: That is so. It is natural that the mind be so inclined to feel future pains so that our present actions be chastened by the implications of our deeds. Fear and Guilt are the heady brews of self regulation without which anarchy and chaos would reign supreme.

Soc.: Are you saying like Alcibiades, that his ever increasing anguish over his behavior was its perfect remedy?

Arist.: I am saying that some measure of anticipatory dread is meet to define our purposes, lest in our felicity we ignore important information that would lend itself to our well being.

Soc.: In what way would your knowing be affected by a lack of unhappiness? Are you saying, again, that what you know you know only through the medium of your miseries?

Arist.: While it is true, my knowing is itself unaffected in any necessary way by pain or pleasure, still, I believe that coloring our knowledge with our emotions is a constant of human activity; it gives to poetry the power to draw forth responses, and without it the world would be pale and lifeless.

Soc.: But when you speak of emotional coloring, is it not true that you speak mainly of unhappiness in its many forms of dread, rage, grief etc.? In what way would your happiness denude the world of color and depth, of wonder and joy, of harmony and peace?

Arist.: The darker hues of painful feelings give depth to the human condition and intensity to the expression of human emotions. One can sense this in our plays and in the response of the populace to tragic events.

Soc.: Are you saying that your comic intuitions are of lesser status? Would you rather not feel the dread that you feel when you think upon my fate and the severity of civil punishments?

Arist.: In truth, it is unpleasant and I would rather it pass from me.

Soc.: Then, like Alcibiades, would it mean anything about you were you not to feel this dread as you ponder my fate or your own?

Arist.: This dread is like a hired mercenary; it keeps me aware of possible danger, but it imprisons me with its presence. Cities that hire mercenaries to defend them often become the victims of their defenders.

Soc.: Why do you believe you have anything to defend yourself against in the first place?

Arist.: I waver on the edge of letting go of what I see as the need to defend myself through my dread; but if I am in error and should suffer some unfortunate turn of circumstance?

Soc.: In what way could you be in error by letting go of your unhappiness?

Arist.: By not knowing something that would be useful for me to know.

Soc.: To repeat the earlier question in a slightly altered form, in what way would your knowing be affected by your happiness? If you grant that your knowing is available to you without reference to your dread, then how is your knowing diminished by being unencumbered by dread?

Arist.: Ah yes, like the marathoner who cuts off a foot to improve his running. Yes, it is clear that to let go of my unhappiness is to trust myself and my knowing. Yes, when I do that, I can glimpse the former dread of your fate and I find it much less painful to contemplate.

Ant.: But, sweet philosopher, I too have my presentiments about this new way of being. Surely you stand the risk of being mocked for giving up the tried and true ways of traditional thinkers and of losing the respect of the populace.

Soc.: Dear cynic, are you saying that you personally would fear being mocked should you accept the way of happiness as your way of being?

Ant.: You know well that there are many who await for any opportunity to discredit you and me for that matter. Yes, I have some reservations about the consequences of accepting such views for myself.

Soc.: What are you afraid would happen were you to let go of these final scruples?

Ant.: That I would somehow be disarmed of reason and subject to folly and the ridicule of my peers.

Soc.: In what way would the experience of happiness disarm your reasoning powers? Again, do you believe that your powers of discernment are enhanced by the clouds of pain and dread in any form?

Ant.: It is a way of thinking that runs deep in my nature, and perhaps in the nature of humankind at large. Upon reflection, I can see that my dread serves no purpose of enhancement of knowing. And, so I can contemplate opening myself up to my felicity without reserve, for if I come to know anything about my world that would help preserve me, I would not ignore it because I was feeling happy. Rather, I would be more attentive to my creatively engaging with it, precisely because my life would mean more to me as a happy existence than as an unhappy one.

Soc.: Excellent old friend, and all of you, let us drink to our good feelings and to a life as filled with them as we dare to make it!

No Pain, No Gain

By now the themes in the Dialogue have become familiar to the reader who has followed the journey through this book. What might be helpful to emphasize are two aspects of the same issue, the believed need to use pain and unhappiness to motivate ourselves and the fear that without our unhappiness we would have no reason to do anything.

The use of our unhappiness as a motivating mechanism of the psyche is perhaps the primary objection raised to happiness on the part of the gate keepers of cultural, religious, ideological moral structures. That is, that to be happy is a static, iconic state, as they see it, which in some sense is a mere pause, a reward to be sure, but it is only the attractor goal that draws seekers of bliss. The real engine that moves and shapes reality is our boiling sea of discontents that keep us ever vigilant, on edge and scourge us by their stinging nettles of intrapsychic and interpersonal rebukes if we dare to remain too long in this alleged stasis of happiness. This quote beautifully describes the labyrinthine pseudo-logic of unhappiness in this way:

When a person is believing he/she has to be unhappy, what they are believing is that they have to be unhappy because they believe they are against themselves. The belief in unhappiness is the belief in being wrong for oneself. Unhappiness, in fact, means that I believe that I do, or want, or think, or feel a way that is bad for me. A person believes: Certain things I do not want to happen may happen or are now happening. I don't want them to. I feel bad (and am worried or afraid now) because I "shouldn't" be thinking negatively about my life now. Maybe I shouldn't be not wanting what is evidently happening anyway. I am (as if) denying reality, and that is wrong. I will be unhappy about this in the future because when certain things I do not want or do not like happen I will feel a way that is bad for me. It is wrong to expect misfortune. That is "unhappy" of me. It doesn't matter that if the undesirable event happens to me from circumstances out of my control, or if I think I am the cause or part of the cause; unhappiness comes as me believing that I now have proof that I am bad for myself.12

As described earlier in our work, it is believed that only by internalizing these painful behavioral boundaries and feelings of inadequacy or unfulfillment can there be a sufficient motivational "vacuum" created that will draw recalcitrant human beings into useful personal and, more importantly for cultural/social purposes, into potent collective actions on behalf of the community. Humans, then, must be kept at a certain level of disease with themselves lest they fall into the indifferent, socially dysfunctional quiescence of felicity!

Alcibiades fears Socrates' death because it could mean the loss of his friend and mentor, one he sees as a motivator to remind him of how he "ought" to be. Without this, he asserts, he would be "rudderless", without the sting of necessary discontent from which to derive a course of action.

It is only when they come to know, as you could as well, that unhappiness is like a mercenary hired to defend against the enemies of sloth, laziness, unwarranted contentment, malaise and foolish fantasy; and, that within short order, as we know from our personal lives, this mercenary becomes our master and not our servant.

Imagine, if you will, standing at the bottom of a mountain and entertaining the notion that you would like to get to the top. As you are pondering this, along comes someone who, divining your desire, offers to help you to get there. You agree to accept the help and this individual immediately leaps on your back and begins to harangue and shout at you to move your worthless ass up the mountain. Let us say you comply and with enormous effort you attain the summit, whereupon this "helpful" individual hops off and declares: "See, you could never have made it without me!"

To illustrate this further, let us take the briefest look at three very popular recently published books about the human psyche and behavior. The first, by M. Scott Peck, entitled *A World Waiting To Be Born: Rediscovering Civility*, quotes from a likeminded Herman Melville: "To scale great heights, we must come out of the lowermost depths. The way to heaven is through hell." This theme is seconded in Peck's vision of therapy: "Psychotherapy is not about happiness; it is about power. If you go the whole route I cannot guarantee that you will leave here one jot happier." Further he says: "the more conscious and healthy and civil you become, the more it will hurt."

Echoing the same vision is Thomas Moore, in his best seller *Care of the Soul: A Guide for Cultivating Depth and Sacredness in Everyday Life*, when he talks of what he calls the "darker side of life" and notes: "Anyone who thinks that life's only goal is happiness will be troubled. The less pleasant parts of life cannot be avoided. If you reflect on your unhappy experiences, you will find that they offer their own gifts…and contribute to the development of your soul." He then goes on to note how such experiences as Depression actually "deepen the personality, leaving you better able to cope with future problems. People who have only seen the sunny side of life may be overwhelmed when something bad happens."

Lastly, in this short overview, let me mention the book *Listening to Prozac* by Peter D. Kramer. The author, a psychiatrist, who lauds the sometimes extraordinary alleged ability of the antidepressant drug, prozac, to alter radically a small minority of its users and bestow upon them a remarkable experience of equanimity and balance. But he then goes on to give us warning of what he considers the danger of such a potential for mood altering. In what amounts to shades of Huxley's *Brave New World* and the artificial bliss inducing substance *soma*, he worries that we are on the threshold of a chemical paradise of happiness, such that no one would be motivated to do anything "naturally" because there would be no disease to provoke them into activity.

Dare I, in a bit of whimsy, suggest that all such cases as the above authors, and legions of the likeminded, are fearful of be referred to my good friend the eminent, world renowned clinical dysphoricist, Dr. Hans Verklempt, who is perfecting his anti-euphoria treatment, the perfect prophylaxsis for those unfortunate souls who totter on the edge of terminal bliss and may fall into the bottomless pit of equanimity—THE HEMORRHOIDAL IMPLANT! Yes, my friends, this highly experimental procedure, though not yet covered by insurance nor approved by the FDA, still bears promise of saving many souls in the throes of felicity. It is said to be capable of producing a high quality of dis-ease and ongoing incremental misery, though a minority of patients seem, most unfortunately, resistant to the effects of the implant. This, has by no means deterred the intrepid Dr. Verklempt who has pledged his life to seeking ever more effective means of dysphoria maintenance. Indeed, he likes to point to himself as an exemplar of what can be accomplished!

This is the metaphoric function of unhappiness; it is thought to be the indispensable spur, the *sine qua non* without which we would presumably fall into an irretrievable soporific stupor of "mindless bliss!" Let me end this chapter with a basic truth, as I see it, about happiness. It resides completely in our ATTITUDE, i.e., the attitude of admitting happiness to be our primary reality. Out of that Attitude came the method. The questions are devised, like Socrates' dialogue, to expose the truth resident in the Attitude. With the Attitude comes everything, the enormous verve of wonder about the world and all the exploration singly and in cooperation with others, as you playfully enjoy the garden of delights that reality becomes when the Attitude prevails in your heart.

Chapter Seven

If You Meet the Buddha on the Road...

This chapter is an exploration of the concept of the self, again, as noted in the very beginning, in the spirit of an understanding of ourselves as self created fictions whose ongoing story either affirms what is, that is happiness, or affirms what is not, unhappiness. Often times, people from other philosophical perspectives will say that this vision is very like their own. Sometimes those who practice the Buddhist way will offer this notion. While respecting the accomplishments of the Buddha and his message, this chapter is devoted to pointing out the differences. For we anchor our understanding of Option as a Method and a Way of Life in the unabashed affirmation of the Self, not as something that is the cause of pain, but as the very entity that creates the landscape of all possibilities, whether that be choosing unhappiness through the architecture of one's beliefs or whether that be admitting happiness as the ground of all that there is or ever could be. Buddhism and the Buddha, then are not singled out as a target, but simply as an opportunity to explain the Option message about the self and about wrongness, suffering and evil. I note, that as with Christianity, there are those who would interpret the teachings and sayings of the Buddhist texts differently, but I am speaking to what is traditionally understood. Let me also note that many quotes from the Sacred Buddhist texts are interwoven with the narrative in various places and I have not specified when that occurs so as not to break the flow of the story.

The so-called understanding that something is wrong or evil in the world solves nothing. It is not an understanding. It is just a restatement of the problem. Peaceful, happy understanding would mean that there is no threat to one's own happiness.... By the way, this fear has led many philosophies and religions to cope by believing that the material universe, or the undesirable aspects of it, is an illusion. Viz. Christian Science, Gnosticism, Shamanism, Witchcraft, Buddhism etc. This way, they are not seen to be against the truth. What they are against is, therefore, false and not reality, but only a deception.13

Meeting in the Wood

Thus have I heard, when the future Buddha was in the Great Retirement and walking on his way to Uruvela to consummate the attainment of enlightenment he came upon a stranger, a foreigner sitting by the wayside at the entrance to a great wood. And the future Buddha, considering it appropriate to rest at this spot, took up a place across from the stranger, who greeted the Buddha thus: "How good it is at last to meet you." To which the Buddha replied: "it is indeed good for us to meet. May I offer you to know the Noble Way, so that you may attain to enlightenment?"

"I am most contented with what I know, but if it pleases you then present to me what you understand as the Noble Way."

"It is wrought from the understanding of what causes pain and misery, and that is the understanding of Dependent Origination, whereby through consciousness comes sensations which in turn breeds desire, which in turn breeds attachment, which in turns breeds existence, which in turn breeds birth and on birth depends old age, and death and sorrow, lamentation, misery, grief and despair."

"Why do you believe that unhappiness arises out of desire?" asked the stranger with a benign smile, his small moustache framing a round face with close cropped hair, much like the Buddha himself.

"Because desire is the vehicle through which the generality of humankind founder and deepen in the folly of attachment."

"What do you mean?"

"Clearly, dear stranger, humans long for so many things, and the pain of that longing without that longing being requited is the illusory fruit of desire. And when desires are requited, as in the pleasures of the flesh, or the achievement of sovereignty, the transitory nature of such experiences breeds despair and disappointment. Thus is desire the root of human misery."

"Are you saying that you personally have experienced unhappiness when you desired something and did not receive it?"

"I have known such unhappiness in my early life when hoped for experiences were not fulfilled, but now I await enlightenment."

"What about not getting what you wanted was distressing for you?"

"Desire breeds distress because what one desires will inevitably be withheld from one in so many instances, and even when gratified, the realization that all that one has achieved or possessed is transitory leaves one depressed and thirsting for what is permanent. Thus have I known such experiences, whether it was the pleasures of the flesh, which are fleeting and depend upon a body that is destined to disease, decay and dissolution or whether it was earthly power, where honors and treasures eventually crumble in the face of time and human limitations. For now we know that birth is misery; old age is misery; disease is misery; death is misery; sorrow is misery; misery is misery; association with those we do not love is misery; separation from those we love is misery; the list is endless in this realm of rebirth and limitation where only lamentation and misfortune hold sway."

"What about things being transitory distresses you?"

"It is in the realm of the transitory that evil is to be found; therefore to avoid evil one must strive to non-attachment to this realm and the evil blossoms of desire."

"What do you mean by evil?"

"By evil is meant all the putrid fruits of illusion that deflect humans from the undying truth of the All. When I was born, the gods decided to make manifest to me this truth in the guise of four visions, one of a miserable aged man, next of a diseased old man, third of a dead body and last of a monk, striving to attain the truths of non attachment. In this fashion, it became clear to me that evil was living in the ignorance of the higher being, and, in this way, are we trapped in the blandishments of the transitory, even as it decays all around us and offends our nostrils with its message of impermanence."

"What about things decaying is offensive?"

"It is a constant reminder of the unavoidable frustration of limited being, of the narrow horizons that are available to those who live in this prison of the passing."

"In what way is living in the limited frustrating?"

"This brings us back to desire, that basic activity of the illusory self; for, out of desire comes yearning, that most intense striving after what will satisfy the true self, but which is captured in the labyrinth created by the web of illusion and led into an endless maze that produces endless longing and endless pain."

"What do you mean when you say "illusory self" and "true self?"

"By Illusory self I mean all form, all sensation, all that is the basis of an Ego or anything related to an Ego, all predispositions whatsoever, all consciousness whatsoever, past, future, or present, be it subjective or existing outside, gross or subtle, mean or exalted, far or near, which is coupled with depravity and attachment. For, all this harkens back to the primary state of ignorance of the All on which depends karma, consciousness, name, form, the organs of sense, contact, sensation, desire, attachment, existence, birth, old age, death, sorrow, lamentation misery, grief and despair. In brief it is that false conjugation of impressions that asserts itself to be something when it is nothing."

"And what of the true self?"

"When all the chain of painful causation is broken, link by link even unto the cessation of ignorance, then one has achieved the end of the noble craving."

"What do you mean by the 'noble craving'?"

"By the noble craving is meant one who perceives the wretchedness of what is subject to birth and craves the summum bonum, the incomparable security of the state of a Nirvana free from birth. When one grasps the fourfold emptiness disclosed in the words 'I am nowhere a somewhatness for any one, and nowhere for me is there a somewhatness of any one.' By this is meant that one has no Ego to bring forth a somewhatness for any one, nor has any one else an Ego to bring forth a somewhatness to him in any role of brother, friend or follower. Thus it is known that there is no Ego anywhere, nor is it possible, therefore to say, 'this is mine; this I am; this is my Ego.'"

"What is wretched about birth and the existence of the Ego?"

"By just observing the human body we see its repulsiveness; even a king is no better than a slave, were he not to clean himself thoroughly, put on the finest raiment, garments of silk and gold, anoint himself with the most fragrant unguents and ornaments; for, only then does he assert himself as an 'I.' But, underneath the facade of perfume, gold and silk, is the body itself, which no amount of adornment can hide; it is a collection of bones and organs covered by a sack of skin, prey to vermin, the seat of disease, subject to all manner of miseries. Through its nine apertures it is always discharging matter like a ripe boil, snot, food, bile, phlegm, blood, faeces, urine, while from the pores of the skin an unclean sweat exudes attracting black flies and other insects. Yet are men so wrapped in blindness and infatuated by a passionate fondness for their own selves, that they believe it to be something desirable, lovely, lasting, pleasant, and an Ego."

"What about the reality of birth, the assertion of the I or Ego and the affection of humans for their bodies and the acceptance of all its functions and exigencies distresses you?"

"While I am now anticipating an existence beyond distress, still, these were the experiences that did distress me and these are the paths that bring confusion to the generality of humankind. They take the changing dance of the senses as true reality and follow it to their ruin and misery. In doing so they bind themselves to the endless movements and changes and sufferings of the recurring cycles of death and rebirths that are of their own causing. They must make the distinction between the discriminative mind, which creates the cycles of birth, pain and death, and that which is un-born and never dies, that which abides within them as the unchanging nature of Mind."

"And if they do not make this distinction between what you call discriminative mind and true mind?"

"It is as I have spoken, they will whirl around in their patterns of painful illusion over countless lifetimes."

"And even if it is as you say it is, what about that? Does this distress you in any way?"

"It is for me to preach the Noble Way and to encourage the Noble Craving that they might escape the iron wheel of destiny and be free to enter into the incomparable state."

"And if your message is not heard or rejected?"

"Such things affect me less and less, but they will affect those in the grip of illusion."

"And these people in the grip of what you call illusion, are they not doing all they know to do based upon what they know at each moment that they act?"

"They are acting in accord with the flow of their illusions, that is true."

"And is that all right with you?"

"My compassion would direct me to continue to bring to them the truth as I have come to know it."

"Yes, but would it be all right with you that humans continue to choose the paths of illusions, despite your message?"

"There is still an edge of distress in my yearning not only for the attainment of full non-attachment but also in wanting others to acquire that blissful state."

"Is there anything you are afraid would happen were you not to be in any distress over the fate of humans or over your own final yearnings?"

"I still have some sense that I would be lacking in true compassion for my fellows were I to surrender this last shred of distress."

"So, is it accurate to say that your way, however attenuated by your coming enlightenment, of making sure that you maintain a sense of your own true compassion is to create your distress so that you will know to be compassionate?"

"Well, stranger, you have anticipated some of the dimensions of true enlightenment, for what you ask does strike a chord in my mind. Still, you seem to balk at accepting the core understanding about the evil of the transitory and its co conspirator in maintaining the value of that illusion, that is the Ego or the discriminative mind."

"Then let me ask you again. You spoke of your yearnings for the eternal as opposed to what you describe as the evil of the transitory and the false conjugation of impressions called the Ego that abet that illusion. What do you mean when you say 'yearnings'?"

"By yearnings, I mean that state of intense movement toward the All that is inspired by a realization of the wretched state of living in a limited state of mind."

"And if your yearnings are not fulfilled, how would you feel about that?"

"This would mean pain and misery as it is for the great mass of humankind who by not achieving the fulfillment of their inner strivings wallow in the endless cycles of birth and death."

"Are you saying that it is inevitable that humans, that you, in so far as you share this view about yearnings, must feel pain and misery at not achieving the object of their strivings?"

"But, stranger, do you not see, that is again at the center of the dilemma of desire and the Ego as its instrument. As I said earlier, unrequited longings in the realm of illusion breed pain and suffering."

"And, again, what about not getting what you desire or long for creates pain and suffering?"

"It is in the nature of humans to be distraught at failing to obtain what they want. This pain is the seed of a wisdom to know that such desires are useless and blinding."

"Are you saying that humans would not want the very best they could know to want unless they were frustrated and suffering over not getting what they desire?"

"Ah, yes, but it is the wanting and the desiring itself which is part of the chain that brings misery."

"Are you saying that humans have no choice about how they are going to feel? Is not your own enlightenment what you have chosen in response to what you believe about the nature of being?"

"Yes, as I have come to discernment about the nature of true mind, I have chosen the noble path."

"Then in what way do humans not choose how they wish to respond to their either getting or not getting what they want or desire?"

"You present your perspective well, stranger. So you are saying that it is not desire and wanting that is the center but the decision to be unhappy about the outcome of desire and wanting that is crucial."

"How do you feel about viewing things in that way?"

"I am not comfortable with such a conception of things, for to legitimize desire would also be to accept the transitory and its medium the Ego."

"And what about accepting them would be difficult for you?"

"The acceptance of the transitory and the Ego for me would mean the acceptance of the pain of limitation as well."

"In what way would that be true for you?"

"By such an acceptance, I would be ipso facto surrendering my inner promptings and yearnings for the All, for the incomparable state of enlightenment"

"Are you saying that your way of making sure that you do not lose touch with your desire for the All is by creating distaste and discomfort at the prospect of accepting the transitory so that you will be certain not to accept it?"

The future Buddha smiled a knowing smile that was reciprocated by the stranger as he answered: "Ahh, so it is that you have shown that my discomfort and distaste is not required for my knowing. I could know that I do not want what is transitory by my knowing without any requirement of discomfort or unhappiness to buttress my knowing or to protect me from my own decisions. Ahh, yes, that is so, stranger, and as others choose according to their attachments to illusion, that is also true. Therefore, there is no inevitability to the painful consequences of desire. Let that be so, then, but the noble path understands that the Ego is still an illusion, for one cannot come to the limitless through the agency of the limited; that which discriminates cannot know that which has no division to be discriminated."

The stranger leaned forward to the future Buddha as he lingered on his words: "My friend, you have come to know that desire does not breed discontent, but rather, the decision to be discontented breeds discontent; you have learned that that decision is indeed based on an illusion, though not the one that you have associated with it; that is, that the generality of humankind believes, as you have believed, that their unhappiness and frustration, misery etc., are somehow inevitable since they believe that all their equanimity depends upon getting what they desire. Thus is the notion of evil born. Evil is the tension between the 'yearning' you describe (with its implications of pain if it is not requited) and the apparent inevitability of not getting what one wants. Further, not getting what one wants brings unhappiness. Now you say that the limited cannot know what is unlimited. Let us see together what actually is. If desire is not the cause of human suffering, then what is transitory cannot be evil, for there can be no evil, that too being a fruit of illusion. If there is no evil, then there is only being, perceived correctly or incorrectly. What would stand in the way of correctly perceiving being?"

"With desire and evil eliminated as a cause of human suffering, then what is left is illusion or what people affirm to be and what actually is not."

"Good, then what is it people affirm to be and actually is not?"

The future Buddha smiled broadly again and responded: "Well, if we are to follow your logic, among the things affirmed to be false are that there is evil and that the transitory is this thing called evil. Further, what is affirmed falsely, based upon the notion of evil, is that desire is evil because it inevitably brings pain both in getting what one wants, which is transitory, and in not getting what one wants, which is frustrating and leads to depression and despair. Neither can the Ego be evil since it is the organizer of the beliefs that create desire in its many forms and there is no such thing as evil, just the affirming of what is. Ahhh, then there simply is what is and humans either affirm that or only believe that they do but actually affirm what is not, i.e., evil, unhappiness etc. in whatever form."

"And what is the seat of such affirmation?"

"The knowing self is the seat of such affirmation."

"And in what moment does the knowing self affirm whatever it affirms?"

"In whatever moment it is in."

"And is not that moment the only moment in which affirmation can take place as you yourself have said, or will say, not in any past, which does not exist, not in any future, which is but hypothesis, and not even in any present, understood as some kind of duration, but only in the eternal now of the actual instant available for such affirmation?"

"As you say it, so it seems to be as I search myself to know the truth."

"In what way is that actual moment limited?"

"By the knowing self's capacity or ability to know?"

"And what limits that ability to know?"

"Ahh, yes, the limitation comes from falsely affirming what is, that is affirming the reality of unhappiness, evil and all consequent notions that give rise to all the miseries of the spirit and the unhappy interpretations of the afflictions of the body."

"And if one were to affirm correctly and be consonant and accepting of that affirmation unconditionally?"

"So, then the knowing would deepen without end as one affirmed and explored all that is."

"So, then in what way would the knowing self be limited in the unlimited eternal now, as you have affirmed it, from knowing the unlimited?"

"Thus in so many ways does your vision coincide with the noble craving for the All, for in that incomparable state, there can be no yearning, no pain, no anger, no frustration, no attachment of any kind."

"Perhaps in some respects this may be true, but a basic question for you is why do you believe, given what you have come to know, that there is any incompatibility with the knowing self affirming what it can know and doing so in the eternal now to whatever depth it wishes given its openness to admitting the fullness of what is?"

Again the future Buddha smiled and replied: "If all there is is what is and there is no chain of dependent origination stretching from ignorance through existence, desire and the ego, then the proper attitude is that of the full acceptance of the All as a reality now in each moment to the degree we choose to affirm it to be so. Then, all is and always was as it was supposed to be and there is no requirement that anything be any different. True compassion is simply the affirmation of what is and the consequent knowing that all, however enmeshed in their illusions, are doing exactly what they know to do, until such time as they may come to know to do something else, perhaps to affirm what is and to admit into their active knowing what is already true whether they admit it or not. Happiness is, and always will be, nor can it be any other way."

The stranger, smiling in a manner that reflected the visage of the Buddha himself stood up and both in a spontaneous reflex embraced each other intensely. After bowing to one another, the Buddha turned his face toward his destination and whatever enlightenment might mean to him now. The stranger stepped back into the wood and vanished into the ages.

Are You Good? Are All Things Good?

What follows, as has been the case with all the quotes in this book (except where noted) are the thoughts of the founder of Option, Bruce Di Marsico. These are particularly apropos of the primacy of the self and the affirmation of happiness as the primary ground of our being. It is a fitting way to end the last chapter of this book:

In the moral sense it would have to follow that everything that is, including yourself, is truly good, in that nothing is bad. If good is better than not bad and is supposed to be a "proof" that you are truly good for yourself, and proof therefore of your right to be happy, then you will need to know that everything is proof of your goodness and holiness; thereby understanding all as causing happiness. Your very being is the cause of your happiness—your right to be yourself is happiness. It is your nature to be good. It is evident that you have the right to be happy, always. You are made that way and have no choice. Since your very self desires happiness above all, and since nothing has the power to deprive you of happiness, you have the ability, because of your right, because you are allowed to be happy. You have no choice but to be yourself. Your self can not be other than good for you, nor can your self act other than in your best interests. Your best interests are anything you want them to be. Your self defines your best interests in the way that you are best satisfied is best. You will always agree with your self as to what your best interest is, and will always be motivated accordingly. You always agree with yourself, perfectly, and never do not. You have no choice. Don't be ashamed of anything you are. You are in perfect conformity with the cause of your being. In religious terms, you are exactly the way God wants you to be, and you need not, nor cannot be otherwise. Do anything or don't do anything, now or at any time. You can never harm or diminish the happiness in your future. You can always expect to be happier and happier. All people are good and can do no evil, but all believe otherwise. All have the right to be happy. They have no choice. To live in joy and peace is the happy reality.14

Conclusion

"Oh Moment Stay!"
(Goethe)

We have traveled through a variety of dialogues, of fictional states and we have reached the end of this work. The quote from Goethe's Faust points to the summation of our vision. Faust was given all that he wanted by Mephistopheles provided that he did not require an attachment to any one moment of his experience, in the sense of requiring the possession of that moment to be happy. When he did, and uttered the words "Oh moment stay," he lost himself.

We could know that each moment is a transformative one and that we do not have to yearn for any other to complete ourselves. We could know that each moment is and always will be utterly unique unto itself, and that it is pregnant with all the untold possibilities that we could create from it. Further, we could know that there is no special information we need to have in order to be happy; that we need no advanced degrees, no special place in time and history, no preeminence among our fellows, no initiation into some secret complex knowledge that requires an endless apprenticeship, no freedom gained by therapeutic exorcisms and absolutions from the terrors, pains and evil alliances of

our parents and all the miscreants of our past; that the great DEMOC-
RACY OF HAPPINESS IS ITS IMMEDIATE AND UNMEDIATED
AVAILABILITY TO ALL WHO WILL ACCEPT IT RIGHT NOW!

That happiness is what is, all that there is, when we simply allow it to
be for ourselves by letting go of our myths of unhappiness. The choice is
not to be happy, but to surrender unhappiness. To do that, in the many
ways we have illustrated in our dialogues, IS to be happy. The dialogue
method spoken about and illustrated in the stories is an invaluable guide
to demythologizing our beliefs about unhappiness, and for many, if not
most, it will be the temporary "Virgil" to guide you out of the "Inferno" of
unhappiness. Reviewing the questions and how they are used in the contexts of these tales is as sure a clinical map to knowing the truth about how
we have created our own illusions of unhappiness as any repetition of
major problems in a standard didactic sense. Though, of course, my other
work *Joywords* offers that option to those who want that approach.
Additionally, my book *The Joybuilding Workbook* or even my novel, *The
Godspeak* can offer a great deal of further insight. So, I do indeed urge you
to do what seems best and live your happiness in the immediate now, even
as you read these words.

Yet, there is a more direct and simple method of admitting your happiness, and remember it is your PERSONAL happiness, your idiosyncratic sense of what that means, not some generic, one size fits all,
version of happiness, but only YOUR SPECIFIC EXPERIENCE!
What I describe now is a paraphrasing of what the discoverer of Option
has described to me.

People are afraid to stop being unhappy because they are afraid they
might be deceiving themselves and only believe they are happy but are
really unhappy. But you didn't get happy by *believing* you were happy but
by *knowing* that you only merely believed you were unhappy. Happiness is
the truth.

You could not make up being happy. *What we call believing we are
happy is merely reflecting the truth of our happiness.* If we don't want to feel

bad, then under what circumstances would we continue to feel bad? Only when feeling bad will stop us from feeling bad! Feeling bad is seen as being honest. Therefore, admitting we feel bad is a way of making sure we can't fool ourselves, so that we won't believe something that is not true. That would be that we might believe we feel happy when we might actually be feeling bad! Ask yourself the following questions as the ultimate shortcut to being and maintaining your happiness:

DO YOU WANT TO FEEL BAD NOW?

IF NOT, THEN DO YOU WANT TO BE HAPPY NOW?

IF YES, THEN NOW DECIDE IF WHAT YOU

JUST SAID IS TRUE! YES? THEN BE HAPPY, MY FRIEND!

What could be more fitting than an exhortation to invest trust in the one person whose trust is crucially meaningful. YOU! Is it not true that you want what you most approve of? How could you not? When you know this and you know this is true, then are you going to lie to yourself? And, finally, if you say that you were convinced beyond any doubt and say that you fooled yourself, then how can you ever convince yourself of anything. This is truly THE UNBEARABLE WRONGNESS OF BEING. Only a messiah or some outside force could possibly SAVE YOU FROM YOURSELF, and MAKE YOU HAPPY AGAINST YOUR WILL! BUT ALAS, EVEN SO YOU WOULD HAVE TO APPROVE OF THIS! Since, no matter how hard you try, you cannot, in ontological truth, abdicate your own deepest nature to be yourself, with all we have seen that implies.

And so I leave you with your decision. If you wish let it be your version of this; that you are who you are *sui generis, svayambhu,* that is, you are self-born, the loving cause of yourself. This is not illusory arrogance. To be is to be happy, is to be free, is to live in the truth. We can do no other whether we admit this or not. But why not have the joy of the Divine by planting your existential flag of being and happiness lovingly in the middle of nowhere, declare it to be somewhere and shout I AM WHO I AM WHO I AM…

Notes

These notes make reference to material that Bruce Di Marsico made available to advanced students of the Option Method. Therefore, since his death in 1995, they are not available as of this writing.

1 All You Need to Know About Your Life. pg.1.
2 Understanding the Option Method. "Unhappiness is Not Wrong." pg. 1.
3 Lecture Notes, 1993.
4 Understanding the Option Method. "Unhappiness is Not Wrong." pg. 2
5 Teachings: A Series of Instructions on the Option Method. "Allowed to Be." pg.1
6 The Basis. pg. 4
7 Teachings: A Series of Instructions on the Option Method. "Choice."
8 The Origin of the Option Method. pgs. 7, 8.
9 The Basis. pgs. 4, 5.
10 The Basis. pg. 4.
11 The Basis. pgs. 13, 14.
12 All You Need To Know About Your Life. pg.1.
13 The Basis. pgs. 11,12. 14 All You Need To Know About Your Life. pg.4.